WORK it OUT!

Compiled by Pat Edwards and Wendy Body

Acknowledgements

We are grateful to the following for permission to reproduce copyright material; Edward Arnold (Publishers) Ltd for the extract 'Sir Gawain & the Green Knight' in *Heroes & their Journeys* by Paul Groves & Nigel Grimshaw; the illustrator's agents for an illustration by Quentin Blake accompanying the poem 'Little Red Riding Hood & the Wolf' in *Revolting Ryhmes* by Roald Dahl (pub Puffin); Jonathan Cape Ltd for the poem 'Little Red Riding Hood & the Wolf' in *Revolting Rhymes* by Roald Dahl & two accompanying illustrations by Quentin Blake (pub Jonathan Cape Ltd); William Collins Sons & Co Ltd for an extract from *The New Noah* by Gerald Durrell; the author's agents for the story 'Eggshell Saturday' by Marjorie Darke in *The Magnet Book of Spine Chillers* (pub Methuen Children's Books), copyright (c) 1981 by Marjorie Darke; MS Magazine Corporation for the story 'The Story of Opal' by Opal Whiteley, adapted by Jane Boulton; the author's agent for the poem 'A Commercial for Spring' in *Jamboree Rhymes for All Times* by Eve Merriam, copyright (c) 1962, 1964, 1966, 1973, 1984 by Eve Merriam. All Rights Reserved; Penguin Books Ltd for an extract from *Plays for Laughs* by Johnny Ball (pub Puffin, 1983), copyright (c) Johnny Ball, 1983 & an extract from *Master of the Grove* by Victor Kelleher (pub Kestrel Books, 1982), copyright (c) Victor Kelleher, 1982; the author's agents on behalf of Joan Fitzhardinge, for the story *When the City Stopped* by Joan Phipson. Pages 12-13 were written by Karin Moffett.

We are grateful to the following for permission to reproduce photographs: Beken of Cowes, page 13 *centre*; English Heritage, page 12 *below left* and *below centre*; Farringford Hotel, IOW, page 12 *below right*; Isle of Wight Tourist Office, pages 12/13 *background*, 12 *above*, 13 *above left*, 13 *below*; Needles Pleasure Park, owned and operated by Leading Leisure plc., page 13 *above right*.

Illustrators, other than those acknowledged with each story, include Azoo pp. 28-9; Chris Meadows pp. 40-1; Rebecca Pannell pp. 42-3, 60-1, 70-5; Lorraine Banks pp. 44-5; Rachel Legge pp. 50-1; Bettina Gutheridge pp. 62-3, 79, 98; Chris Meadows pp. 94-5; John Fairbridge pp. 96-7.

Contents

I still think I'd see a doctor if I were you!

FULL OF EASTERN PROMISE

by Johnny Ball

Cast of characters (in order of appearance):

SLAVE
QUEEN DIANA, THE SULTANA OF ABADANA
MAID
WASSI WAROO, THE WASSIER
IYAM, THE JAILER/PRINCE MUSSPI

The setting is an Arabian palace with lots of cushions covering a bench or chaise longue. Here, QUEEN DIANA, THE SULTANA OF ABADANA *reclines eating a bunch of grapes. She is attended by a* SLAVE *who has a large ostrich-feather fan. (This could be made of paper.) The* SLAVE *waves the fan continuously with one hand while in the other (or even attached to his leg) he has a large drumstick with which he bangs a huge gong. (Huge gongs are very rare and expensive, but you could make something that looks like a gong and have someone in the wings banging a cymbal close to a microphone for the effect.) Each time the gong is struck, everyone on stage vibrates until the noise dies down.*

[*The gong sounds. Curtain opens.*]

SLAVE: Hello, Cor, what a job this is. Standing here all day waving this fan. You see, I'm the chief wave slave. Every waft causes a draught so that makes me the chief draught wafter. On top of all that, I have to bong the gong so I'm chief gong bonger too. So there you are—chief wave slave, draught wafter and gong bonger...and all for her, Queen Diana, the Sultana of Abadana. She eats grapes all day, but she'd rather have a banana.

SULTANA: Oh, where is my son? My long lost son, Prince Musspi? He left the palace twenty years ago on his bike just to get some

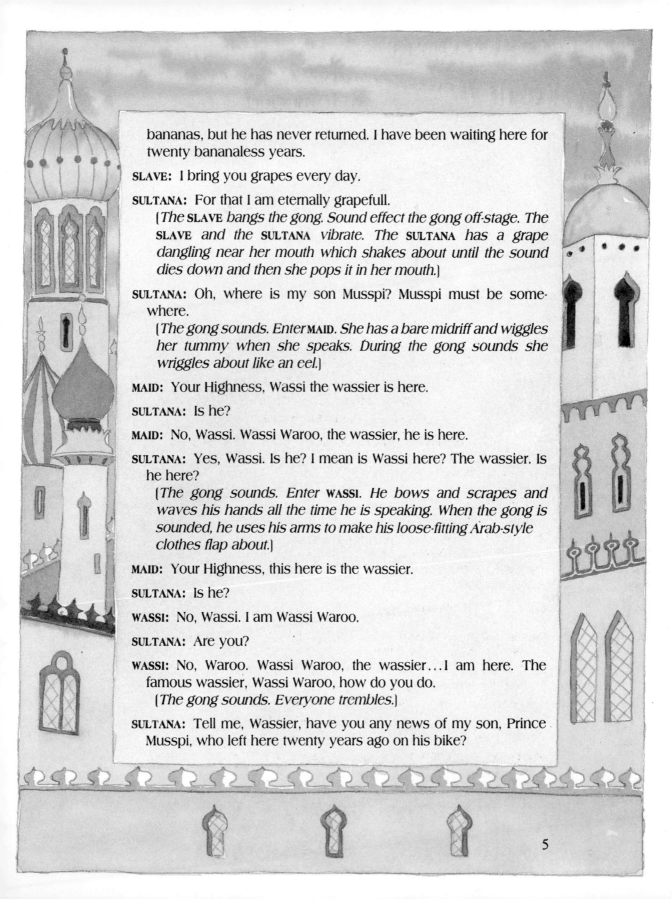

bananas, but he has never returned. I have been waiting here for twenty bananaless years.

SLAVE: I bring you grapes every day.

SULTANA: For that I am eternally grapefull.
  [*The* **SLAVE** *bangs the gong. Sound effect the gong off-stage. The* **SLAVE** *and the* **SULTANA** *vibrate. The* **SULTANA** *has a grape dangling near her mouth which shakes about until the sound dies down and then she pops it in her mouth.*]

SULTANA: Oh, where is my son Musspi? Musspi must be some-where.
  [*The gong sounds. Enter* **MAID**. *She has a bare midriff and wiggles her tummy when she speaks. During the gong sounds she wriggles about like an eel.*]

MAID: Your Highness, Wassi the wassier is here.

SULTANA: Is he?

MAID: No, Wassi. Wassi Waroo, the wassier, he is here.

SULTANA: Yes, Wassi. Is he? I mean is Wassi here? The wassier. Is he here?
  [*The gong sounds. Enter* **WASSI**. *He bows and scrapes and waves his hands all the time he is speaking. When the gong is sounded, he uses his arms to make his loose-fitting Arab-style clothes flap about.*]

MAID: Your Highness, this here is the wassier.

SULTANA: Is he?

WASSI: No, Wassi. I am Wassi Waroo.

SULTANA: Are you?

WASSI: No, Waroo. Wassi Waroo, the wassier…I am here. The famous wassier, Wassi Waroo, how do you do.
  [*The gong sounds. Everyone trembles.*]

SULTANA: Tell me, Wassier, have you any news of my son, Prince Musspi, who left here twenty years ago on his bike?

5

WASSI: Your Highest Highness, I have consulted the sands of the desert in which all knowledge is writ…

SULTANA: What rot.

WASSI: Rot? 'Tis not rot. 'Tis right.

SULTANA: 'Tis right? That in the sands all knowledge is writ?

WASSI: Right.

SULTANA: Well then, who wrote what is writ?

WASSI: The spirits writ it.

MAID: It's not writ…it's wrote.

WASSI: The spirits wrote it.

SULTANA: Wrote what?

WASSI: Wrote what is writ.

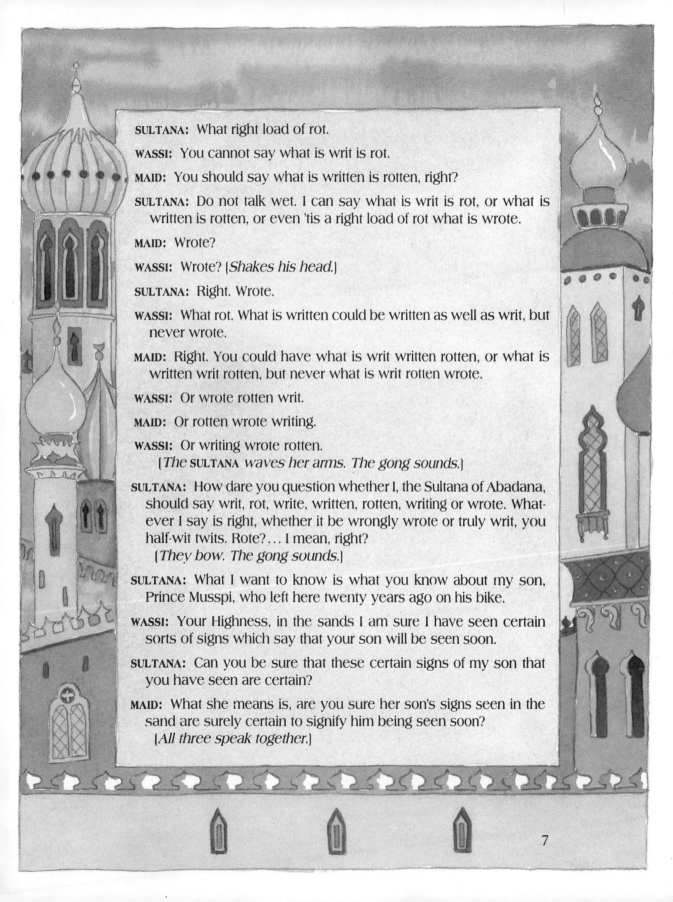

SULTANA: What right load of rot.

WASSI: You cannot say what is writ is rot.

MAID: You should say what is written is rotten, right?

SULTANA: Do not talk wet. I can say what is writ is rot, or what is written is rotten, or even 'tis a right load of rot what is wrote.

MAID: Wrote?

WASSI: Wrote? [*Shakes his head.*]

SULTANA: Right. Wrote.

WASSI: What rot. What is written could be written as well as writ, but never wrote.

MAID: Right. You could have what is writ written rotten, or what is written writ rotten, but never what is writ rotten wrote.

WASSI: Or wrote rotten writ.

MAID: Or rotten wrote writing.

WASSI: Or writing wrote rotten.
[*The* **SULTANA** *waves her arms. The gong sounds.*]

SULTANA: How dare you question whether I, the Sultana of Abadana, should say writ, rot, write, written, rotten, writing or wrote. Whatever I say is right, whether it be wrongly wrote or truly writ, you half-wit twits. Rote?… I mean, right?
[*They bow. The gong sounds.*]

SULTANA: What I want to know is what you know about my son, Prince Musspi, who left here twenty years ago on his bike.

WASSI: Your Highness, in the sands I am sure I have seen certain sorts of signs which say that your son will be seen soon.

SULTANA: Can you be sure that these certain signs of my son that you have seen are certain?

MAID: What she means is, are you sure her son's signs seen in the sand are surely certain to signify him being seen soon?
[*All three speak together.*]

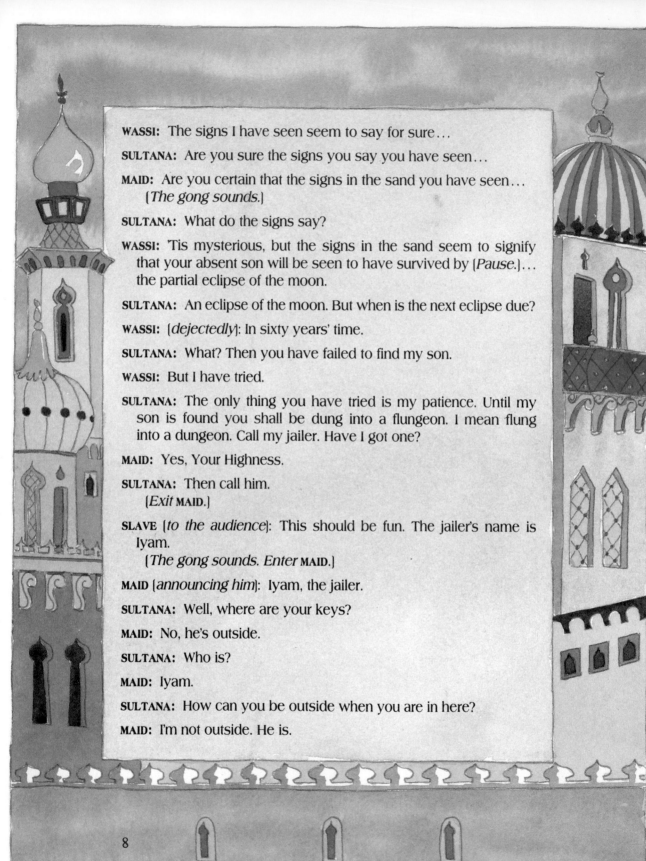

WASSI: The signs I have seen seem to say for sure…

SULTANA: Are you sure the signs you say you have seen…

MAID: Are you certain that the signs in the sand you have seen…
[*The gong sounds.*]

SULTANA: What do the signs say?

WASSI: 'Tis mysterious, but the signs in the sand seem to signify that your absent son will be seen to have survived by [*Pause.*]… the partial eclipse of the moon.

SULTANA: An eclipse of the moon. But when is the next eclipse due?

WASSI: [*dejectedly*]: In sixty years' time.

SULTANA: What? Then you have failed to find my son.

WASSI: But I have tried.

SULTANA: The only thing you have tried is my patience. Until my son is found you shall be dung into a flungeon. I mean flung into a dungeon. Call my jailer. Have I got one?

MAID: Yes, Your Highness.

SULTANA: Then call him.
[*Exit* **MAID.**]

SLAVE [*to the audience*]: This should be fun. The jailer's name is Iyam.
[*The gong sounds. Enter* **MAID.**]

MAID [*announcing him*]: Iyam, the jailer.

SULTANA: Well, where are your keys?

MAID: No, he's outside.

SULTANA: Who is?

MAID: Iyam.

SULTANA: How can you be outside when you are in here?

MAID: I'm not outside. He is.

SULTANA: Who is?

WASSI: Iyam.

SULTANA: You are in here.

WASSI: The jailer is outside.

SULTANA: Is he?

WASSI⎫
MAID⎭ [*in unison*]: No. Iyam.

[*The gong sounds. Enter* JAILER. *He is wearing pantaloons with bicycle clips. He has a large bunch of keys which rattle when the gong is struck. He is a bit dim.*]

SULTANA: Who are you?

JAILER [*slowly*]: Iyam…

SULTANA: Go on.

WASSI: Iyam the jailer.

SULTANA: You are the prisoner.

JAILER: Is he?

SULTANA: No, Wassi. Wassi Waroo. Who are you?

JAILER: Iyam, the jailer.

SULTANA: Well, where have you been?

MAID: He was outside.

SULTANA: Was he?

MAID: No, Iyam.

SULTANA: Is he the jailer?

WASSI: Yes. Iyam.

SULTANA: You're Wassi.

JAILER: Is he?

SULTANA: No, Wassi. Who are you?

JAILER: Iyam, the jailer.

SULTANA: Is he?

WASSI
MAID   (*in unison*): No! Iyam.
JAILER

    (*The gong sounds.*)

SULTANA: Oh, I feel dizzy. Right, *You*—lock *him* up and don't let him out till you see a partial eclipse of the moon.

WASSI (*drops to his knees grovelling*): Oh, no. Don't lock me up. People will say, "Wassi, Wassi! Oh, where is he?" Or, "Wassi Waroo, where are you?"

SULTANA: Take him away.

WASSI: Wait.

JAILER: Ten stone four.

WASSI: No. Not weight, wait. What are these? (*Pointing to* **JAILER'S** *ankles.*)

JAILER: They're my bicycle clips.

WASSI (*rising to his feet*): Then what was writ was not total rot, just wrongly writ.

SULTANA: Don't start that again.

WASSI: But Your Highness, don't you see? 'Tis the sign. 'Tis the sign.

SULTANA: What, the partial eclipse of the moon?

WASSI: No—the bicycle clips of your son.

SULTANA: Then he must be…

WASSI: Musspi.
    (*The gong sounds.*)

MAID: Iyam?

SULTANA: Not you, him. He was my son all the time.

MAID: Was he?

WASSI: No, Iyam.

JAILER: I am Iyam.

MAID
WASSI } [*in unison*]: No, Iyam!

JAILER: No, I am.

SULTANA: No. You were Iyam, but now you are Musspi and the owner of all the riches in this kingdom.

JAILER: I am? Then Iyam…must be…Musspi.
[*The gong sounds. The cast wobbles downstage and forms a line*—SLAVE, MAID, WASSI, SULTANA, IYAM.]

ALL: [*in rhyme*]: We hope everyone has enjoyed all the fun
In our tale about Wassi Waroo.
And just in case you were a little confused,
We'll try to explain who was who.
[*Each character points at whoever they are talking about but looks either to the front or to the others.*]

MAID: Now Iyam, her son.

WASSI: No, you were the Maid.

SULTANA: Iyam's mother and Musspi's was me.

SLAVE: Yes, Iyam the jailer and Musspi the son,

JAILER: They were one and the same and both me.

SULTANA: Now he was the slave.

MAID: Oh, was he? I see.

WASSI: It was I who was Wassi, not you. [*Pointing to the slave.*]

SULTANA: Yes, he was the slave,

SLAVE: Yes, she was the Maid,

MAID: The Sultana was you…
[*Slight pause.*]

ALL: Toodle-oo.
[*The gong sounds.*]

CURTAIN

Illustrated by Azoo

11

The Isle of Wight

At twenty-three miles long and thirteen miles wide, the Isle of Wight is England's largest island, with sixty miles of coastline. The island is separated from the mainland by the Solent, a stretch of water from one to six miles wide.

For over 2,000 years the island has been under threat of invasion. First the Romans, who called the island 'Vectis', then the Saxons, Danes and French. There were fears that the Spanish Armada would land on the Isle of Wight but the fleet was defeated at sea.

The Needles

The world's first permanent radio station was built on the cliffs at Alum Bay by Guglielmo Marconi in 1897.

Hundreds of ships have been wrecked off the island's rocky coast and the caves and deep inlets made it ideal for smuggling.

The Needles are three giant chalk rocks rising out of the sea at the western tip. There was once a fourth rock which crashed into the sea during a storm in 1764.

Carisbrooke Castle

Osborne House

Farringford House

In 1647, King Charles I was held prisoner in Carisbrooke Castle, south of the island capital, Newport. After two unsuccessful escape attempts he was finally taken to London and executed in January 1649.

Queen Victoria's husband, Prince Albert designed Osborne House and they lived here for over two months each year. Her nine children played in a Swiss Chalet built in the grounds. The Queen died at Osborne in 1901.

The Victorian Poet Laureate, Alfred Lord Tennyson lived at Farringford House which is now a hotel.

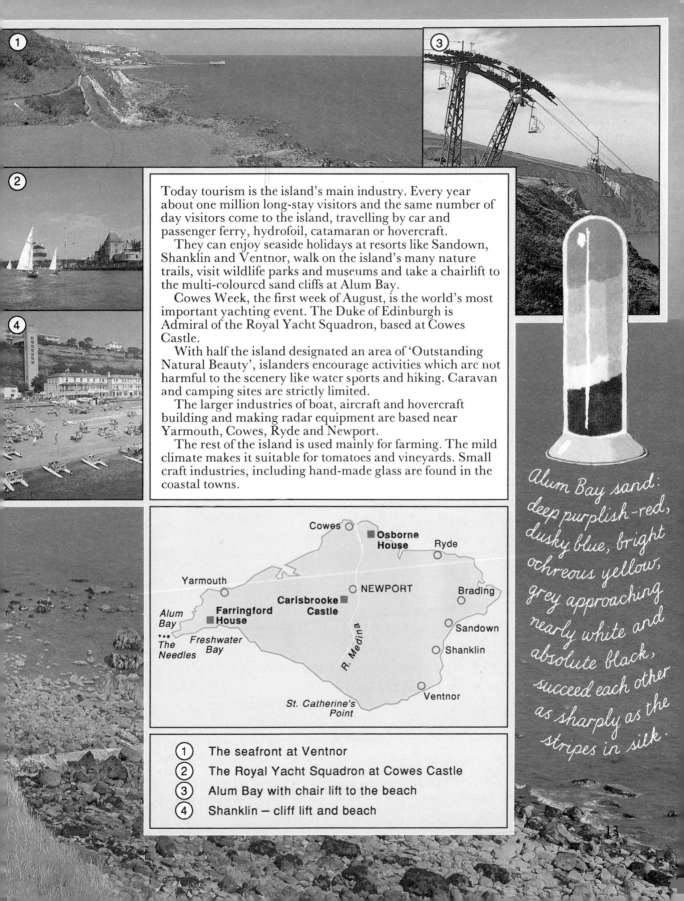

Today tourism is the island's main industry. Every year about one million long-stay visitors and the same number of day visitors come to the island, travelling by car and passenger ferry, hydrofoil, catamaran or hovercraft.

They can enjoy seaside holidays at resorts like Sandown, Shanklin and Ventnor, walk on the island's many nature trails, visit wildlife parks and museums and take a chairlift to the multi-coloured sand cliffs at Alum Bay.

Cowes Week, the first week of August, is the world's most important yachting event. The Duke of Edinburgh is Admiral of the Royal Yacht Squadron, based at Cowes Castle.

With half the island designated an area of 'Outstanding Natural Beauty', islanders encourage activities which are not harmful to the scenery like water sports and hiking. Caravan and camping sites are strictly limited.

The larger industries of boat, aircraft and hovercraft building and making radar equipment are based near Yarmouth, Cowes, Ryde and Newport.

The rest of the island is used mainly for farming. The mild climate makes it suitable for tomatoes and vineyards. Small craft industries, including hand-made glass are found in the coastal towns.

Alum Bay sand: deep purplish-red, dusky blue, bright ochreous yellow, grey approaching nearly white and absolute black, succeed each other as sharply as the stripes in silk.

Map labels:
Cowes · Osborne House · Ryde · Yarmouth · NEWPORT · Brading · Carisbrooke Castle · Farringford House · Alum Bay · The Needles · Freshwater Bay · R. Medina · Sandown · Shanklin · St. Catherine's Point · Ventnor

1. The seafront at Ventnor
2. The Royal Yacht Squadron at Cowes Castle
3. Alum Bay with chair lift to the beach
4. Shanklin — cliff lift and beach

13

Eggshell Saturday

Snap! That's how it seemed to happen. Almost quicker than it takes to say. One moment it was a perfectly ordinary summer Saturday, with the traffic going along Slater Street and old Ma Bagley weighing sweets behind the counter and scratching her nose like always, then the next ... the next was unbelievable!

"What d'you want, duck?" Ma Bagley asked him.

"*Beano* please, and six of them Sports Jellies," Leroy said. He took the comic and watched her pick out two tennis rackets, three motorbikes and a football. She'd got weird hands, he noticed. Fat, with knobbly knuckles and rings stacked up each finger. There was even a ring on one thumb. And a single hair grew from the mole on her chin.

"Fourteen pence, duck," she said.

Leroy paid and went out of the shop sucking a tennis racket and reading about Dennis the Menace who was after the Softies in boxing gloves this week. Crazy! He chewed, wanting to read on, but decided he couldn't *and* push a pram. Not if he wanted to steer straight. Reluctantly he dropped the comic on the pram quilt and kicked off the brake, looking at the quiet mound that was Rosa. At least she'd drifted off to sleep and wasn't roaring any more. With luck she'd still be sleeping when he got her back home. That would please Bernice. He smiled, thinking of a particular black and yellow leather soccer ball in Chapman's window. He'd saved all but a quid towards it and felt convinced he'd earned at least the loan of that final quid by getting Rosa to shut up.

He pushed the pram down Slater Street, past the hole in the road where a workman was mending the gas mains, past Bones's the undertakers, past the Indian grocer's, to the library, and was just going to turn the corner when he heard a shout.

"Leroy ... hey, Leroy ... wait, can't you!"

He knew that voice. Mandy Philpotts! For a brief moment he thought he'd do a ton-up job with the pram. Mandy Philpotts was a fat nit and would want to gawp at the baby. She'd pull back the cover and that would set Rosa off again, and that would mean Bernice would be mad, and *that* would mean no quid.

"Hey, Leroy, is that your baby brother?" Mandy came panting up, long hair in rats' tails over her shoulders, flat feet slapping on the pavement. She was lugging a couple of library books.

"Rosa's a girl, not a boy, and she's my sister's kid," he said coolly, adding with pride: "I'm her uncle."

"Cor!" Mandy was obviously impressed. "How old is she?"

"Eight weeks and two days."

Mandy homed in. "Let's have a look then."

"No. You'll wake her up and then she'll bawl."

"I won't. You see. I'll be ever so gentle," and before he could stop her she had peeled back the quilt.

"*Cor!*" she said again, and a puzzled look spread across her face.

Leroy didn't notice. He was too occupied staring down at the small baby still peacefully asleep in the pram. Rosa's bonnet all right. Rosa's woolly jacket with the blue ducks and blue buttons. Rosa's shawl his Nan had crocheted. But the baby inside wasn't Rosa. No way! He blinked hard as if that might put things right. But it didn't make any difference. Ice beads came from nowhere and lay along his spine. Something clutched and squeezed his stomach.

15

"Thought you said she was your sister's kid?" Mandy said.

He didn't know how to answer. Couldn't *think*. All he knew was what he could see. There in the pram lay a baby so pale, so ash white, it might never have seen the sun.

At that moment the baby woke up. Glass green eyes stared steadily at Leroy. An old cold look. The ice beads joined up so he felt as if he was shut inside an iceberg.

"I mean, this baby isn't even *brown*," Mandy said accusingly.

"Shurrup!" Leroy put on an act of anger. "You've woken her up. Didn't I say you would? She'll bawl now. You see!" He shoved the quilt back into place and began pushing the pram at a furious speed round the corner and along the main street towards the Ring Road without heeding the direction. Panic covered every thought in his head except making a getaway. Just as suddenly he stopped as another thought walloped him. He mustn't let Mandy shove off. Her tongue was as long as a bog roll. Give her half a chance and it would be all round town before you could say Juliet Bravo about Bernice's kid changing colour.

He swung the pram round, trembling.

Mandy was staring after him as if he'd lost his marbles! He called to her:

"Hang about!"

It felt like hours before he got back to the corner and he still hadn't pulled his thoughts together. He blurted out:

"Don't go. I want to talk to you."

"What about?"

He didn't answer directly. "I'm going to the park. Wanna come?" And with a burst of inspiration: "You can push if you like."

She grasped the pram handle. "Is it okay if I put the books in?"

He nodded and gave her a motorbike to suck to stop her chatter while he got his brains in order. Think . . . *think*, he told himself.

People nicked kids from outside shops. He'd read so in newspapers. But he'd never read of a swap. And that's what this was. Must be. Somebody had nicked Rosa and her pram, somebody else had parked a fresh pram, and he had nicked the new kid by accident. A swift look told him not to be so daft. He'd know that scratch by the hood anywhere. But as a double check he squeezed up his eyes, imagining the outside of Ma Bagley's. *There had been only one pram, and it had been standing exactly where he had left it.* The inescapable fact was so shattering that when Mandy asked, "Is that really your sister's kid?" he said, "No!" before he could catch the word.

"W hose then?" Mandy asked, turning in at the park gates.

Leroy didn't answer. He was struggling with a feeling of nightmare. Prams didn't dart about like dodgem cars. Babies didn't change colour. Picture fragments kept popping in and out of his mind. Bernice screaming and weeping. His Nan going bananas. All the neighbours crowding into the kitchen for a look at the bleached baby. And knocking on the front door, the biggest beefiest copper in the world . . . come for *him*!

"You all right?" Mandy asked, slowing down and looking at him anxiously.

He gulped and licked dry lips, trying to stop panicking.

Just then the baby woke again and began to wail.

Jeepers, that was all he needed! He felt sick.

The wails grew.

"Poor little thing." Mandy bent over the pram. "Maybe she's hungry. Is it her feed time?"

"No. She had a bottle before we came out." He knew straight away that this was nonsense. "I mean, Rosa did," he added miserably.

Surprisingly, instead of shooting out another stream of questions, Mandy lifted the baby from the pram, and laying it against her shoulder, rubbed its back. The baby burped twice very loudly, stopped crying and gave Leroy a wide crooked smile.

"Thought so," Mandy said. "Wind. Just like our Billy. Force nine gale he is after his feeds. Both ends."

But Leroy wasn't listening. Every hair on his arms, every hair on his neck, stood erect as corn stalks. He sucked in a rapid breath. "It's got *teeth*!" he gasped.

"What's new about babies having teeth?" Mandy slid the woolly bundle into the crook of her arm. A small fist escaped from the shawl.

Leroy knew now with absolute certainty that this was his Nan's shawl. Crocheted to her special pattern, with the rainbow colours running together like melted ice-cream. But how could it be? His bewilderment increased. He watched Mandy tuck a finger into the little waving fist, which straightway stopped waving and made for the tiny bunched mouth.

Then . . .

"Ow . . . ooowww!" Mandy snatched away her hand, staring in disbelief at the pinpricks of blood ringing her finger. "*It bit me!*"

The baby gave a contented coo and blew a few frothy bubbles, then smiled again, revealing two rows of sharp little toothy triangles.

"Told you it had teeth," Leroy muttered, feeling no satisfaction at all in being right.

Mandy had gone almost as grey pale as the baby. Hastily she dumped it back in the pram. Leroy quite expected her to grab her books and bolt, but she lingered.

"Whose baby did you say?" she asked in a voice like sandpaper.

"I didn't. All I know is it's wearing our Rosa's things whoever it is." Despair made him reckless. "I was only in old Ma Bagley's shop for a couple of minutes. There just wasn't time for our Rosa to get nicked. Nor no people to do it."

They stared at one another. Mandy coughed. Opened her mouth. Closed it again. Opened it. "I've been reading," she said hoarsely.

Leroy, who had been hoping for something more constructive, snapped: "Big deal!" rather crossly.

"About changelings." She coughed again and slid him a sideways look.

"What?"

"Changelings . . . faeries swapping their babies for humans."
Her gaze moved to the pram. Leroy's followed.

"You have to be joking."

"No, I'm not."

And she wasn't. He could see that she was dead serious.

"Knickers!" he said, not to needle her, but because he really thought she'd slipped her trolley and needed straightening out.

"Okay, you think of a better explanation. Everything fits." She sounded tart as crab apples. "Here, look . . ." and seizing one of the library books, began thumbing through until she found the page she wanted, thrusting it at him.

He took it and read: "From many countries come folktales of babies being snatched from their cradles and faery changelings put in their place. It is said that the faeries are envious of the beauty of human babies, and . . ."

Mandy interrupted: "I bet Rosa's pretty, isn't she?"

Leroy thought of Rosa's plump dusky cheeks, her big dark eyes, the soft fuzz on top of her head, her lovely toothless grin. He felt an awful pang of loss. "Yes."

"There you are then!" She was triumphant. "So all we've got to do now is get her back. Tells you how. Read that story," turning a page and pointing.

Leroy began to feel as if he was swimming in treacle. Nothing made sense and he couldn't get anywhere. Now was now, with jet planes, and robots making cars, and micro chips, and his Nan working in Tesco's. All this stuff Mandy was dishing out about faeries swapping babies was a load of crap. Surely she couldn't expect him to *believe*? And yet . . .

He took another quick nervous look at the chuckling baby. Holy cow! Those teeth had saw edges like a bread knife. Weirdo skin colour, too. And the look on its face was sort of . . . *knowing*. His own skin tingled and shrank. Hurriedly he went back to the book. Opened his mouth to read.

"NO!" Mandy bellowed. Leaning close, she whispered: "*It*'s got ears. If you read out the instructions, *it*'ll know and the trick won't work."

The nightmare feeling grew. Silently he focused on the story.

"Then the faery child betrayed itself, saying: 'I have seen a thousand winters and a thousand springs and travelled the world while the hills grew old, but never until this day did I see eggshells brewed on the hearth for the table'."

He had a quick vision of himself stewing eggshells in Bernice's enamel saucepan with the flower decorations, on Bernice's brand-new Tricity cooker, while the bleached baby lay in Rosa's carry-cot on the table. He nearly said 'Knickers' again. It wasn't on! Bernice would do her nut. Besides, there wasn't any hearth in Bernice's all mod-cons kitchen. Only a central heating radiator.

He explained tersely into Mandy's ear.

She was quiet for a moment, but not defeated. "There's another bit about *them* living underground. All you have to do is find their front door and cook the thingies outside it."

"Don't you think it would be easier just to wheel the pram down to the Welfare and let them sort it out?" He tried a joke — a last go at keeping his marbles.

"They aren't going to believe anything you say," Mandy told him coldly. "They'll see the teeth and think the baby's a freak and take it to hospital . . . or a kids' Home. Either way, your sister won't get no baby back at all."

"Okay, okay." He wilted under all this reasoning, but still couldn't resist a mild scoff. "Where's this front door then? In a fairy mushroom ring?"

"Middle of town? Don't be daft!" Her face suddenly brightened. "Tell you what, there *is* a ring in town."

"Oh yeah! Where?"

"The Ring Road. Bit of a sweat to find the middle, though. The space is huge. Practically all the town."

With the nasty feeling he was about to prove himself as loony as she was, Leroy said: "If we had a map we could find the middle easy. Draw a circle round the Ring Road with compasses. Make arcs. Lines across and bingo . . . there's your middle." The neatness of the idea pleased him. He smiled a smug smile.

Mandy was impressed. "That's ace!" She began listing all the things they would need. Enthusiastically ticking them off on her fingers. "Map pencil compasses thingies saucepan water matches paper sticks. I should think midnight 'ud be about the right time."

"*Midnight*?" His smug satisfaction crumbled. "Where'll we hide till then? Bernice'll have the cops out long before that."

Mandy gave the problem some thought. "I suppose you could come round to my place. Mum and Dad have taken our Billy to me Auntie Mary's in Birmingham and won't be back till tomorrow. There's only me Gran at home and she's as deaf as a bean bag. Just so long as she don't see you it'll be okay. There's everything we need in our house."

Now that the moment had come for decision, Leroy was silent. The plan was mad. He would be mad to follow it up. He shut his eyes tight. Shook his head to clear it. Flicked up his eyelids and bent over the pram. The nightmare did not go away, and the ash-grey baby gave him a bleak stare. No smile. He shivered, sensing a spite that had nothing to do with the warmth and cuddliness of ordinary babies. Summer sun beat down on his head, but the green stare had him trapped in an arctic frost and was trying to gouge out his thoughts. Forcing him to reveal the secret.

With a huge effort he pulled away, and nodding at Mandy because his voice seemed frozen, grabbed the pram and hurried towards the far gate.

Except for one hairy half hour when a neighbour brought back a borrowed quarter of tea and stayed to help Mandy's Gran drink some of it, the plan went smoothly. They saw no one and were seen by no one, and parking the pram in Mandy's garden shed, crept up into her bedroom. Even the baby obliged by remaining quiet until teatime. Then it began to moan.

"We dunno when it last had a meal," Leroy said. He didn't like it, but faery or not, it had a body and bodies needed grub.

"Haven't got a bottle handy. D'you think it would like bread and milk?" Mandy asked. "We could spoon it in."

The baby seemed content with this arrangement, its teeth making little unpleasant scraping shrieks on the metal.

"It could mince up a steak no trouble," Leroy said. "It don't need slops!" He went back to the map spread out on the floor and began to draw lines across it using Mandy's rule. When he had finished, they both stared at the result.

"Just by the library," Mandy breathed.

"No it ain't. Don't you *see*?" Leroy took the compasses and set the point in the precise middle of the crossing lines. "Bones's."

"I'm not going to Bones's at night," Mandy quavered. "All them coffins."

"Coffins can't hurt you," Leroy said.

"There's stiffs inside 'em ... and *ghosts*."

"A stiff can't hurt neither and ghosts is nothing but see through air." Leroy was far from feeling as brave as his words. He didn't want to ferret around in the undertaker's yard either. But much more than that, he didn't want to be saddled with a baby that was the next best thing to a Kenwood mincer. "You can't back out now," he hissed.

They were tottering on the edge of a quarrel and might have fallen in if Mandy's Gran hadn't chosen that moment to call her from the bottom of the stairs.

"I'll have to go or she'll be up," Mandy said. "I'll be quick as I can."

She took a very long time. It was half past nine by the bedside clock before the door opened and she slipped back in. "Had to stay and watch telly," she said, not meeting his eyes.

He knew she was as scared as he was, but being so pleased to see her didn't say he knew she'd stayed away on purpose.

At a quarter to twelve they picked up the baby and plastic bag they had already packed, and leaving Gran peacefully snoring, went out into what should have been a quiet dark starlit night. But they had forgotten the street lamps and the fact that it was Saturday. Pub and disco night. The whole world seemed on the move. Cars; motorbikes; people on foot; cycling. They narrowly missed being seen from a Panda car — ducking into a jetty. No cars there, but always the risk of meeting someone head on with no escape route.

It didn't happen and they reached the library, coming past the school railings, then, in the shadow of the telephone box which edged on to Slater Street, stopping — horrified!

For there, between Bones's and Ma Bagley's, lay the hole in the road. Since Leroy had passed it that morning, a nightwatchman's hut had been erected. In front, warming his hands at a brazier, sat the nightwatchman. No way could they get into Bones's now. No way could they boil eggshells on the pavement.

Checkmate!

Or was it? Leroy turned an idea over in his mind as the brazier glowed and the kettle on top sizzled and sang.

"If we could just drop the eggshells in there," he muttered.

"You nuts? With him watching?" Mandy whispered scornfully.

A pause.

"Suppose you was to go up to him and pretend you was lost," Leroy suggested casually.

"I live round here. You *are* nuts."

"I said *pretend*. He'd have to help, wouldn't he? Take you …"

"… to the cop shop? Oh, great! I wouldn't half get a telling off when they found out."

Orange street lamps burned steadily, spreading a curious greenish white light, sucking daytime colours from bricks, telephone box, their clothes, their faces as they stared first at each other, then (as if pulled by a magnet) down into the pram. Pale in sunshine, the small face above the quilt now had the waxy look of a corpse. But the eyes lived and burned with such green malice that the breath was stolen from their mouths. They panted as if they had been running hard. Throats turning dry. The eyes grew bigger and more compelling. Two green prisons.

Without a word, dragging her feet, Mandy shuffled towards the old man crouched over his fire.

"Mister," she croaked. "Please, mister …" A sob of real fear broke from her.

Released, Leroy saw the old man look up. Saw rather than heard their conversation and Mandy's tears. The nightwatchman put a comforting arm round her shoulders. Their footsteps echoed and passed him. Left him to the empty, lonely street.

Leroy sweated. Clumsy with fear, he emptied the plastic bag on the pavement, scattering the contents. The eggshells slithered out of their paper bag. Hastily he scrabbled together a small handful, and dragging the pram after him, rushed to the glowing brazier. A split second to lift the kettle lid. Another to drop in the shells.

Somewhere his other self was aware of a searing pain in his hand, but the voice wiped it away. A shrill voice, scaly and brittle.

"Sheep's eyeballs under the Arab stars. Bird's nest soup in Chinese bowls. Roman snails picked with a pin. But never shells boiled in an English kettle … never … never …" The words shattered in a shriek of laughter.

Leroy looked towards the pram. It was rocking violently, hood down, baby upright and clinging to the sides with claw fingers. The waxy face was creased into a laughing lace of wrinkles, mouth agape, saw-teeth glinting — first sharply, then blurred. He couldn't see properly and blinked hard. Everything had suddenly gone out of focus.

T he pram appeared to hover as if the ground had stepped away, then began to roll forward on its platform of air. He watched with horror as the barriers shielding the hole dissolved like sugar in water. There was nothing he could do. His arms and legs were rigid and refused to budge. On the very brink of the hole the pram slowed, teetered, tipped. A wisp of smoke drifting up from the underground depths coiled and shaped into a huge grasping hand, the smudgy fingers stacked with rings. Two indistinct lamps rose above the hole's rim. Leroy blinked again. No, not lamps . . .*eyes*! Briefly everything focused in sharp detail. Eyes in a face; face with mole on chin; mole with solitary hair growing from it. He knew that face, didn't he? The thumb ring, he knew that? Swift as thought the picture edges doubled, trebled. Colour and shapes merging as the glowing brazier, street lamps and eyes were extinguished. There was a deafening CRACK, as if the road had split from end to end.

The sun switched on.

Leroy parked Rosa's pram at an angle under the window of Ma Bagley's shop. He had chosen the spot as a treat. Rosa could now see a row of pink sugar Snoopys. As he kicked on the brake he was still trying to settle which comic to choose. He put out a hand to push open the shop door, and winced. Looking down, he saw that each fingertip had a watery blister.

B listers?
Still puzzling, he went into the shop.
"What d'you want, duck?" Ma Bagley asked him.
He made his decision. "*Beano* please, and six of them Sports Jellies."

Written by Marjorie Darke
Illustrated by Patricia Moffett

27

AWAY WITH THE FAIRIES ......

1 WHAT ARE FAIRIES*?

They're diminutive, supernatural beings, shaped like human beings but endowed with magical powers.

2 WHERE DOES THE WORD 'FAIRY' COME FROM?

The word 'fairy' came into use sometime after medieval times. It then usually referred to mortal women who had acquired magical powers. These women would visit a household when a child was born, and predict the baby's future. 'Fairy' originally meant 'fai-erie', which means 'a state of enchantment'.

3 HOW MANY DIFFERENT KINDS OF FAIRIES ARE THERE?

Take your pick! Gnomes, pixies, dwarves, elves, goblins, leprechauns, brownies, even gods, sprites and fauns are all part of the fairy world. All these whimsical little creatures pop up in the folklore of countries all over the world.

4 WHAT DID FAIRIES DO?

Anything and everything! Some were mischievous, others helpful. Some were good, whilst others were naughty and bad. Some lured human beings into Fairyland, never to return, whilst others stole human babies to rear as their own.

Sometimes spelled faeries

FASCINATING FAIRY FACTS

5 WHY DID FAIRIES STEAL?

It seems that fairies felt they had a right to any human possessions, especially food, and it was believed they only stole things that they felt people didn't deserve to have. However, the fairy folk weren't all bad. Many times they simply borrowed things and were very scrupulous about returning the borrowed item.

6 WHAT WERE CHANGELINGS?

One of the oldest belief about fairies, is that they liked to possess human children. Thefts of babies by fairies were mentioned hundreds of years ago in medieval books. Usually they stole an unchristened child or simply a lovely healthy baby and left a squawking, grizzling impostor in its place. It was believed that the 'impostor' was an unwanted sickly fairy.

7 WHY DID PEOPLE BELIEVE IN FAIRIES?

Hundreds of years ago, anything unusual that happened could, very conveniently, be blamed on the fairies. They were the scapegoats of the day. Most people then lacked education and, in their ignorance, the blaming of bad fairies for a sickly child, poor quality butter, or missing people, made sense to them. Unfortunately, because of their beliefs the people would indulge in some bizarre remedies.

We're innocent until proven guilty!

Beware: *Dip into fairies for two minutes and you'll be gone for an hour...*

No light at all...

Thirteen year old Nicholas Lorimer and his eleven year old sister, Belinda, are alone in their Sydney flat. Things are not normal. For a start, the city has no electricity. Nick is vague about the reasons for this — something to do with strikes and troubles with a nuclear reactor, he thinks, not having listened properly to the explanation at school. Mrs Piggott, the family's daily help, does not usually leave before their mother's return but today, inexplicably, Mrs Lorimer has not returned. Nick has assured Mrs Piggott that he and Belinda will be all right on their own, not knowing that his mother is lying unconscious in a city hospital, her bag with all her identification in it irretrievably lost in the accident that put her there.

For a time in the flat all seemed normal. It was unusual for Mrs Lorimer to be late, but they did not doubt that she would come. Their dinner would turn up as inevitably as Christmas and the night and bedtime would come too. And as Mum was the controller of the daily routine she would naturally be there to tell them to go to bed. Neither of them ever went until told.

Afternoon light still poured in at the windows. Far below people walked and traffic moved. A small breeze ruffled the tops of the plane trees that lined the street. And at the end of the street the harbour opened out, wide and bright. It was no longer as calm as it had been. The breeze was disturbing the surface of the water now and the hard glitter had come back. The white sails of the little boats had filled, and they were being puffed briskly home to their moorings. There were fewer speed boats, though the ferries were busy with homing city workers. They, at any rate, still functioned normally. Across the harbour all the windows of the houses facing west had turned blood red.

Nicholas, who had been looking out of the window instead of doing his homework, turned away. The glory was gone. He was not yet worried about his mother, but too much looking at too wide a view had made him uneasy. Friendliness no longer abounded and in its place had crept a faint hostility.

Binkie was doing her homework after all. "The TV's on the blink," she said as he sat down beside her. "I'll get this done now so I can watch it later when Mum's fixed it."

He nodded, and pulled his own books towards him. For a time their heads were bent over their work. Their breathing became laboured with the agonies of thought. Outside the window the sky paled. Long shadows crept through the streets below. The windows on the other side of the harbour turned from red to pearl and faded from sight as the sun slid down behind the ranges in the west. The street quietened as people went, one by one, in at their own doorways. The breeze, lifting the curtains as it came through the open windows, blew some of the evening shadows in with it.

Nick's nose had been sinking nearer and nearer to the page of his book. "Turn the light on, Binkie, will you?" he said at last.

Belinda tipped her chair sideways and reached for the switch on the lamp beside her. There was a click, but there was no light.

"Everything's gone wrong," said Nick and went over to the door to switch on the main light. That would not go on either.

"See, they've turned the electricity off because of the nuclear reactor," said Belinda. "They told us at school."

"I know all that," said Nick. He did not know because he had not been listening, but he never cared to be put right by Belinda. He went back to the table and sat down. Now that the daylight was leaving the flat there seemed to be an aching space where their mother ought to have been. It was no use trying to work any more. There was no light to work by.

"I expect the car's broken down or run out of petrol or something," said Nick. "She's probably walking home along the street." The image of his mother in the street outside was suddenly so vivid that he got up and went to the window again.

The street was strangely dark. Only the tops of the moving plane trees, a darker grey among the many shadows, were at all clear. Although the rumble of city traffic was not as loud as usual, it was still difficult to pick out footsteps on the footpath. Now and then a car came along the street, shining its headlights along the black tar, and then it was sometimes possible to see if anyone moved under the trees. But it seemed to Nick that the street was empty. No light yet came from the windows of the nearby blocks of flats and the mauve-red glow of the city lights was absent. Instead, the darkening sky hung brooding not far above the highest buildings.

Nick felt a slow tightening of muscles somewhere in his middle, and a heavy emptiness crept into the depths of his stomach. Yet, oddly, he was not hungry. He was leaning with one hand on the sill. The other hung down beside him. As he stood there, uneasy, unhappy and confused, the hand at his side was slowly clutched in a warm and wiry grip. Belinda stood beside him, her face looking up into his, her eyes very wide and her expression — yes, he saw that the self-assurance, the cockiness was gone. It was a frightened face that he saw and the expression showed a kind of question. For once she had nothing to say. For once, she turned to him.

32

Nicholas never accepted responsibility if he could help it. He never entered into competitions that he could avoid. He did not want to be popular, or top, or the best. He liked being left alone. But his parents had seen to it that he had a well-developed sense of duty, and nature had seen to it that his feelings were receptive and acute. And now he knew that Belinda was his responsibility. After all, she was beloved, if aggravating.

His hand tightened round her fingers. "I'll look after you, Binkie," he said, almost in spite of himself.

They stood together for a little while at the open window. But the developing night was not like an ordinary night. Nothing looked the same as usual; nothing sounded the same as usual. The cars whose headlights illuminated the street as they passed looked lonely and hunted, as if they were hurrying to the shelter of their garages. Once, a group of people came along the footpath, and Nicholas thought his mother might be with them, but they passed the entrance to the flats, almost as if they expected something to spring out of the doorway as they went by. And they did not speak at all, but the sound of their footsteps, hurried and clattery, rose up to the open window. The sky above the darkened city was now quite black, but stars were scattered through the blackness, shining their small beams down to the emptying streets.

"I don't like it," said Nick, and drew back, shutting the window as he did so. "Pull the curtains, Binkie."

The furniture and the objects in the room had still been visible when they went to the window. Now there was nothing but blackness. Not even a reflected gleam of brass or silver. But the smell of home, which up to now they had not thought about at all, enveloped them with security and calm. The smell of furniture polish, strong after Mrs Piggott's activities, the fainter smells of smoke and soap and perfume and lingering food smells from the kitchen wrapped them round with comfort.

"We must find a light," said Nick.

"I'll get the torch by Mum's bed," said Belinda and he heard her cross the room, bumping into chairs and tables as she went.

Presently a thin beam of light flashed, wavering, through the doorway. The objects in the room sprang into existence, eager to prove they were still there after all. The light grew brighter and Belinda came into the room behind it. "We better find that lamp Mum bought for the blackout," she said as she came towards him.

"What blackout?"

"Well, there wasn't one, but Dad thought there was going to be so she bought it. Remember?"

Nick remembered, and he remembered for the first time that day that he had a father. He wished it was not next week but this week he was due back. A father was what they needed at this moment. "We better look for it then," he said. "Bring the torch into the kitchen."

It was not as hard to find as they had expected and, better still, there was a box of matches beside it. This reminder of his mother's careful ways gave Nick a sharp and unexpected pang. He had not thought of her for at least a quarter of an hour. She might have come home at any one of those fifteen minutes, but she had not, and the hope within him of her immediate return began painfully to shrivel.

They lit the lamp and put it on the sitting room table, and the first lapping waves of a tide of apprehension that might yet engulf their minds receded for the time being. The first move towards dinner was usually to tidy up their school books and take them off the table. Always they waited to be told by Mrs Lorimer. Tonight, in silence, they packed them up and put them to one side.

"We better find something to eat," said Nick.

They found a pool of water on the floor of the refrigerator when they opened the door. Two butter papers and some old cooked peas were floating about in it. There was a slight foody smell.

"It hasn't really gone wrong, Nick," said Belinda. "It's just the electricity's stopped — like they said."

So they took out what they wanted and shut the door again, as Nick had an obscure feeling that the less they tampered with it the better. It was the same with the television set. They tried it once more and then, faced with the dead and uncooperative screen, let it alone. There was no point in trying the radio either, and neither of them thought of the small transistor radio beside their mother's bed.

After they had taken their plates back to the kitchen they sat for a while alternately watching the steady yellow flame of the lamp and looking at the books they had pulled out of the shelves. But it was hard to concentrate. The room was very quiet and still, and now that they were themselves sitting quietly, the front door began once again to intrude on their thoughts. They were very conscious of it, facing them across the hall. Any moment it might open and their mother might walk in. But it remained shut, and in its refusal to open and admit Mrs Lorimer it became a kind of enemy. Because it remained shut it was keeping their mother out.

Nick had managed to read half a page without looking at the door when he heard a small sound, and saw that Belinda's book had slid off her knee. Her head drooped and her eyes were closed. He put down his own book and got up.

"Come on, Binkie. It's time you went to bed. I'll bring the light."

At any other time she would have refused. She never took orders from Nick. This time she got up without speaking and followed him into the bedroom. He sat on the bed in his mother's room while she cleaned her teeth and got into her pyjamas. He looked at the smooth pillow and found it impossible to imagine that Mrs Lorimer's head would not be resting on it at some time before tomorrow. When Belinda was in bed he went through to her room, pulled up her blankets as he had seen Mrs Lorimer do, and picked up the light.

"Good night, Binkie," he said. "I think I'll wait up for Mum. Call if you want anything." He did not see her eyes follow him as he went out of the room.

He put the lamp back on the table, picked up his book and sank back into his chair. Suddenly the telephone rang. The book slithered to the floor and he was at the telephone, wild with hope, before it had rung three times. It was a wrong number, but when he had recovered from his disappointment it gave him an idea and he settled down to ring as many of his mother's friends as he could remember. None of them had any information to give him. But one lady suggested he should telephone the police. They all told him it was going to be a very difficult time — whatever they meant by that — and at least two of them told him to telephone them again if he and Binkie were in trouble. He thought they were in trouble already, and it seemed to him that he was already telephoning. All of them sounded edgy and unsettled. He tried the police but gave up after twenty minutes of nothing but the engaged signal. He did not want to ring the police anyway. He did not want to think it might be necessary.

He returned to his chair. After trying to read for another half hour he turned the light low and just sat — with his eyes on the front door. Outside the flat, the city was very quiet. The usual night traffic noises had dwindled to nothing. In the silence he twice heard the police siren, but that was all. It was a comfort in a way to know that they were about. After three quarters of an hour his eyes closed, his muscles relaxed and the anxieties of the day were stifled in sleep.

He opened them again many hours later because he was cold. His head ached and he shivered. The lamp still burned, but its light seemed to have paled. He looked round the room and saw that a hesitant daylight was filtering through the curtains. The room, with the window shut and the lamp burning, was very stuffy. He crawled out of the chair, yawning, and went on unsteady legs to the window. Pulling back the curtains he flung it open. The day had come. A white, shadowless light showed an empty street, blank windows and shut doors. Down beyond the end of the street the water of the harbour was white too. No light reflected from it yet and no boats floated on its surface. It waited, as it waited every day, for the sun to rise. Below him he saw the plane trees, their wide green leaves hanging still. And down the street, near the corner, a white cat crossed from one side to the other, taking its time, looking neither to right nor left. At this hour cats, not cars, were the users of the city streets.

He drew back from the window and tiptoed across the sitting room, down the passage, towards his mother's room. His heart thumped. Now she must be there. The new day had come. It was time to start the ordinary daytime routine. He must have slept a long time and she would not have noticed him curled up in the chair. As he drew near the door the breath in his body seemed to be all in his throat — a smothering ball of air unwilling to go either in or out. He stopped, pushed the door a little wider open and looked across to the bed. The disappointment hit him like a sandbag in the stomach. He had to make an effort to stop himself sinking on to the floor. But somewhere in the back of his mind he had known she would not be there.

He looked into Belinda's room. She was asleep, her mouth slightly open and one hand hanging, palm up over the side of the bed. The sight of her lying there oblivious and peaceful sent a wave of jealousy through him. Not fair. And he needed her company. Even Belinda's company he needed now. He stepped across to wake her, perhaps roughly. But then he stopped. Waking her so that she could feel the way he felt did not make sense. He stood looking at her for a few seconds with envy but without resentment and then tiptoed back to the sitting room.

by Joan Phipson
illustrated by Donna Gynell

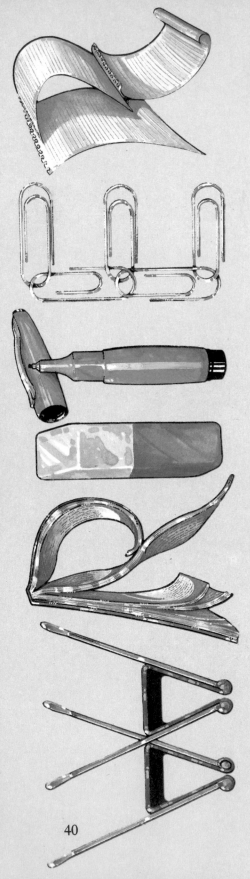

Name: _Joan Phipson_

Born at: _Sydney_

Born on: _16ᵗʰ November 1912_

Started school at: _Bombay_

Favourite subjects at school: _English and History_

What I didn't like about school: _Dress-up parties_

Favourite food when young: _Sausage and mash_

Favourite food now: _Sausage and mash_

Best-loved story or book when young: _The Jungle Book – Kipling_

Favourite kind of books now: _Well written fiction and biography_

Three things I love: _Reading, travelling, walking_

Three things I hate: _Political meetings, snakes in the garden, tripe._

author Joan Phipson

Secret wish: _??????? _

Favourite riddle or joke: _Unsuitable for tender ears and eyes_

Ethnic background — parents: _English_

— grandparents: _English and German_

Autograph: _Joan Phipson_

Joan Phipson invented me!

HEY – TURN ON

Now that's a real disaster!

Where was Moses..

In the d stupid

Where was Moses when the light went off?

Everyone knows the answer to that hoary old riddle.

But it's no joke when the electricity is cut off and we're reduced to stumbling around in the dark, hunting for torch or candle and matches. What's more, it's a bit scary because we've all got so used to electricity just being there like water in a tap. Suddenly — no light, no power to boil water, make a piece of toast, work the TV . . .

Impossible to imagine life without it, isn't it? Yet the use of electricity is a pretty recent invention. You've only got to go back to the 1880s to find a time when there were no electrical appliances at all. Which might seem like ancient times to you, but considering the fact that people have been around for thousands of years, that's just like yesterday.

WHAT TOOK THEM SO LONG?

Yeah, I was wondering that.

Knock Knock

Alex.

Alex Pl Later.

There's no easy answer to that. Like all other inventions it was a gradual process. Each inventor building on the work of others who went before.

To start with, no one had to invent electricity itself. It has always been there. It's an elemental form of energy, something that helps hold the whole universe together. Everything (including you and me) consists of minute particles called 'atoms'. These atoms are made up of tiny specks of negative electricity called 'electrons' which are held together by a central band of positive energy. The unit of positive energy is called a 'proton'. Currents of electricity are found both in the crust of the earth and in the atmosphere and are closely linked with the earth's magnetism.

Amazing, isn't it?

It's electrifying.

42

THE LIGHT!

What did one magnet say to the other magnet?

I find you very attractive.

The unit of magneto-motive force is named after him.

Early people were well aware that there was some mysterious force about, even though they couldn't work out what it was or where it came from. They puzzled over the way the iron they'd invented attracted certain bits of rock. They noticed that their amber beads made fabric or straw cling to them after they'd been rubbing against the wearer's clothing all day. They also noted that spinning distaffs made of amber did the same to the scraps of material. This amber was a fossilised vegetable resin that was most attractive when highly polished, so it was often made into jewellery and ornaments. It was used by early doctors and chemists when they were mixing drugs. What they didn't realise was that it was easily electrified through friction, so that really what they were doing was creating static electricity. But it was because of the amber connection that, in around 1600, William Gilbert (who was physician to Queen Elizabeth) coined the name electricity from the Greek word for amber — *elektron*.

Who's ere?

Ex who?

Frankenstein knew, though!

Meanwhile, it never occurred to anyone that this electricity could be related to those terrifying flashes that split the heavens from time to time. At first, the world's scientists thought there must be several different forms of power involved but eventually some bright sparks began to make a few connections. However, it took a particularly inventive American to light the way. Benjamin Franklin was pretty sure there had to be a link. So one stormy June day in 1752, Ben decided to go fly a kite. Yes, that's what he did. He made himself a kite from light wood and one of his large silk handkerchiefs and went out to see if it was possible to get sparks from the end of a kite cord if you flew it in the middle of a violent thunderstorm. Sure enough, he proved his point, though it proved a somewhat shocking experiment. (Sorry, couldn't resist that.)

Now they had a name and some idea of what the stuff was. Next questions were: "How can we harness this power?" and "What could it do for us?"

I thought was going to be Alex Tricity!

I always said you could get a real charge out of flying a kite!

43

Who invented THE LIGHT BULB?

1 Mid to late 1600s
(Germany) Otto von Guericke, 1602–1686.
First to show the mysterious force could
produce light.
(England) Robert Boyle, 1627–1691.
First to discover electricity can be stored.

2 1752
(United States) Benjamin Franklin,
1706–1790, conducts his famous kite
experiment. He also invents the lightning
rod.

3 1800
(Italy) Alessandro Volta, 1745–1827, invents
the first true electric battery and produces a
steadily flowing current of electricity. The
word 'volt', used to describe the unit of
electromotive force, comes from his name.

'Watt', meaning a practical unit of electrical power, was named after Scottish inventor and engineer James Watt.

4 1809
(England) Humphrey Davy, 1778–1829, invents an electric arc lamp. However, as no
generators or other economical sources of electric power have been invented yet, it's
just thought of as a scientific curiosity. (Davy also invents the miner's safety lamp.)

5 1825
(England) William Sturgeon, 1783–1850, invents an electro magnet.

6 1827
(France) André Marie Ampère, 1775–1836. Chief published work (Ampère's Law of
Electromagnetism) appeared in 1827.

7 1831
(England) Michael Faraday, 1791–1867, devises a simple electric motor and invents the
first dynamo. He becomes known as the founder of the science of electromagnetism.

8 1841
(United States) Engineer named Starr invents a lamp which produces a light by sending
an electric current through a very fine piece of carbon which grew so hot it became
incandescent (that means white or glowing with heat). It burnt out quickly, though.

16 1925

(United States) Marvin Pipkin produces the first commercially successful incandescent lamp to be frosted on the inside.

15 1897

(Germany) Walter Hermann Nernst devises an electric metallic-filament lamp that needs no vacuum and only consumes half the power of earlier filaments.

14 1886

(United States and elsewhere) The electrical industry is now firmly established.

13 1879

(United States) Thomas Edison, 1847–1931, produces a fine wire from little strips of burned or carbonised bamboo. This glows brilliantly with the heat produced when an electrical current passes through it. (These very fine carbon wires become known as 'filaments'.) He encloses them in a glass bulb and creates a vacuum by removing the air. Without oxygen, the filament does not immediately burn away. Hey, presto — a light bulb! Another inventor, Englishman Joseph Wilson Swan comes up with a similar idea, but he uses a thread of chemically treated cotton.

12 1878

(United States) General Electric Company organised to develop and produce incandescent lamps.

11 1876

(United States) Centennial Exposition in Philadelphia, Pennsylvania, exhibits all the electrical wonders of the day. Star attraction is Alexander Graham Bell's telephone. ("Of no real practical use" sniffed the great minds of the day.) But there were also two direct-current generators on display — one designed by Gramme of Belgium, the other invented by an American named Wallace.

10 1869

(United States) Western Electric Company starts in Cleveland, Ohio. It makes telegraph instruments, gas lights, bells, fire and burglar alarms.

9 1841–1869

(United States) Experiments with incandescent lamps continue.

What did the light bulb say to the switch? You turn me on!

45

Her problem seemed solved.

Aha! Ripe, fresh grapes — just what I want!

But alas, these grapes had been grown on unusually high frames.

How on earth am I going to reach?

She found a ladder.

Darn it! Still out of reach!

The fox sat down to think.

Come on, pudding head, there must be a solution!

Thinking's hard work!

Looks like it!

47

So she tried to knock them down, first with a stone...

Those grapes are not just a stone's throw away!

PLOP

...then with a long stick.

Sticks and stones may break your bones but grapes will never feed you!

Another inch maybe!

She tried lassoing them with a piece of old rope.

Ride 'em! Rope 'em! Brand 'em!

Head 'em up! Move 'em out!

48

And she tried a catapult.

SPLOONG!

Reload! The enemy scattereth!

Yep! Missed again!

Finally she hunted around till she found a couple of car seat springs.

But that didn't work either.

And a very angry, disappointed fox gave up in disgust

Moral

People pretend to despise the things they cannot have.

And that's why when somebody criticises something you've done or just got, another friend or member of the family will probably say, "Take no notice. It's just sour grapes!"

49

The Story of CHOLMONDELY

Gerald Durrell is one of those people who seem to know from their earliest years what they are going to be when they grow up. Youngest brother of a gifted, highly original and harum-scarum family, he spent several youthful years on the island of Corfu, off Greece, and was fascinated by the birds, beasts and insects of the island: the tale is told in "My Family and Other Animals", from which you can see that Gerald was bound to become some sort of naturalist. He has made a profession of collecting wild animals around the world, and—what is surely no less important— telling us all about them in delightful books. The present story comes from "The New Noah", in which he shares with young readers some of his African experiences when collecting beasts for his "ark".

When Cholmondely*, the chimpanzee, joined the collection, he immediately became the uncrowned king of it, not only because of his size, but also because he was so remarkably intelligent. Cholmondely had been the pet of a District Officer who, wanting to send the ape to the London zoo, and hearing that I was collecting wild animals in that region and would shortly be returning to England, wrote and asked me if I would mind taking Cholmondely with me and handing him over to the zoo authorities. I wrote back to say that, as I already had a large collection of monkeys, another chimpanzee would not make any difference, so I would gladly escort Cholmondely back to England. I imagined that he would be quite a young chimp, perhaps two years old, and standing about two feet high. When he arrived I got a considerable shock.

A small van drew up outside the camp one morning and in the back of it was an enormous wooden crate. It was big enough, I thought, to house an elephant. I wondered what on earth could be inside and when the driver told me that it contained Cholmondely I remember thinking how silly his owner was to send such a small chimpanzee in such a huge crate. I opened the door and looked inside and there sat Cholmondely. One glance at him and I realized that this was no baby chimpanzee but a fully grown one about eight or nine years old. Sitting hunched up in the dark crate, he looked as though he were about twice as big as me, and from the expression on his face I gathered that the trip had not been to his liking. Before I could shut the door of the box, however, Cholmondely had extended a long, hairy arm, clasped my hand in his and shaken it warmly. Then he turned around and gathered up a great length of chain (one end of which was fastened to a collar round his neck), draped it carefully over his arm, and stepped down, out of the box. He stood there for a moment and, after surveying me carefully, examined the camp with great interest, whereupon he held out his hand, looking at me inquiringly. I took it in mine and we walked into the marquee together.

* *Pronounced Chum-lee*

Cholmondely immediately went and seated himself on one of the chairs by the camp table, dropped his chain on the floor and sat back and crossed his legs. He gazed round the tent for a few minutes with a rather supercilious expression on his face, and evidently deciding that it would do he turned and looked at me inquiringly again. Obviously, he wanted me to offer him something after his tiring journey. I had been warned before he arrived that he was a hardened tea drinker, and so I called out to the cook and told him to make a pot of tea. Then I went out and had a look in Cholmondely's crate, and in the bottom I found an enormous and very battered tin mug. When I returned to the tent with this, Cholmondely was quite overjoyed and even praised me for my cleverness in finding it, by uttering a few cheerful "hoo hoo" noises.

While we were waiting for the tea to arrive, I sat down opposite Cholmondely and lit a cigarette. To my surprise, he became very excited and held out his hand across the table to me. Wondering what he would do, I handed him the cigarette packet. He opened it, took out a cigarette and put it between his lips. He then reached out his hand again and I gave him the matches; to my astonishment, he took one out of the box, struck it, lit his cigarette and threw the box down on the table. Lying back in his chair he blew out clouds of smoke in the most professional manner. No one had told me that Cholmondely smoked. I wondered rather anxiously what other bad habits he might have which his master had not warned me about.

Just at that moment, the tea was brought in and Cholmondely greeted its appearance with loud and expressive hoots of joy. He watched me carefully while I half-filled his mug with milk and then added the tea. I had been told that he had a very sweet tooth, so I put in six large spoons of sugar, an action which he greeted with grunts of satisfaction. He placed his cigarette on the table and seized the mug with both hands; then he stuck out his lower lip very carefully and dipped it into the tea to make sure it was not too hot. As it was a trifle warm, he sat there blowing on it vigorously until it was cool enough, and then he drank it all down without stopping once. When he had drained the last drops, he peered into the mug and scooped out all the sugar he could with his forefinger. After that, he tipped the mug up on his nose and sat with it like that for about five minutes until the very last of the sugar had trickled down into his mouth.

I had Cholmondely's big box placed some distance away from the marquee, and fixed the end of his chain to a large tree stump. He was too far away, I thought, to make a nuisance of himself but near enough to be able to watch everything that went on and to conduct long conversations with me in his "hoo hoo" language. But on the day of his arrival he caused trouble almost as soon as I had fixed him to his tree stump. Outside the marquee was a lot of small tame monkeys tied on long strings attached to stakes driven into the ground. They were about ten in number, and over them I had constructed a palm leaf roof as a shelter from the sun. As Cholmondely was examining his surroundings, he noticed these monkeys, some eating fruit and others lying asleep in the sun, and decided he would have a little under-arm bowling practice. I was working inside the marquee when all at once I heard the most terrific uproar going on outside. The monkeys were screaming and chattering with rage, and I rushed out to see what had happened. Cholmondely, apparently, had picked up a rock the size of a cabbage and hurled it at the smaller monkeys, luckily missing them all, but frightening them out of their wits. If one of them had been hit by such a big rock, it would have been killed instantly.

Just as I arrived on the scene, Cholmondely had picked up another stone and was swinging it backwards and forwards like a professional cricketer, taking better aim. He was annoyed at having missed all the monkeys with his first shot. I grabbed a stick and hurried towards him, shouting, and, to my surprise Cholmondely dropped the rock and put his arms over his head, and started to roll on the ground and scream. In my haste, I had picked up a very small twig and this made no impression on him at all, for his back was as broad and as hard as a table.

I gave him two sharp cuts with this silly little twig and followed it up with a serious scolding. He sat there picking bits of leaf off his fur and looking very guilty. With the aid of the Africans, I set to work and cleared away all the rocks and stones near his box, and, giving him another scolding, went back to my work. I hoped that this telling-off might have some effect on him, but when I looked out of the marquee some time later, I saw him digging in the earth, presumably in search of more ammunition.

Not long after his arrival at the camp, Cholmondely, to my alarm, fell ill. For nearly two weeks he went off his food, refusing even the most tempting fruit and other delicacies, and even rejecting his daily ration of tea, a most unheard-of occurrence. All he had was a few sips of water every day, and gradually he grew thinner and thinner, his eyes sank into their sockets, and I really thought he was going to die. He lost all interest in life and sat hunched up in his box all day, with his eyes closed. It was very bad for him to spend all day moping in this fashion, so in the evenings, just before the sun went down, when it was cool, I used to make him come out for walks with me. These walks were only short, and we had to rest every few yards, for Cholmondely was weak with lack of food.

One evening, just before I took him out for a walk, I filled my pockets with a special kind of biscuit that he had been very fond of. We went slowly up to the top of a small hill just beyond the camp and then sat there to admire the view. As we rested, I took a biscuit out of my pocket and ate it, smacking my lips with enjoyment, but not offering any to Cholmondely. He looked very surprised, for he knew that I always shared my food with him when we were out together. I ate a second biscuit and he watched me closely to see if I enjoyed it as much as the first. When he saw that I did, he dipped his hand into my pocket, pulled out a biscuit, smelled it suspiciously, and then, to my delight, ate it up and started looking for another. I knew then that he was going to get better. The next morning he drank a mugful of sweet tea and ate seventeen biscuits, and for three days lived entirely on this diet. After this his appetite returned with a rush, and for the next fortnight he ate twice as much as he had ever done before, and cost me a small fortune in bananas.

There were only two things that Cholmondely disliked. One of them was the Africans and the other, snakes. I think that when he was a baby some Africans must have teased him. Whatever the reason, however, he certainly got his own back on more than one occasion. He would hide inside the box and wait until an African passed close by and then he would rush out with all his hair standing on end, swinging his long arms and screaming in the most terrifying manner. Many a fat African woman carrying a basket of fruit on her head would chance to pass too closely to Cholmondely's box, and would have to drop her basket, pick up her skirts and run for dear life, while Cholmondely danced victoriously at the end of his chain, hooting and showing all his teeth in a grin of delight.

With snakes, of course, he was not nearly so brave. If he saw me handling one, he would get very agitated, wringing his hands and moaning with fear, and if I put the reptile on the ground and it started to crawl towards him, he would run to the very end of his chain and scream loudly for help, throwing bits of stick and grass at the snake to try and stop it coming any closer.

One night, I went to shut him up in his box, as usual, and, to my surprise, he flatly refused to go into it. His bed of banana leaves was nicely made, and so I thought he was simply being naughty, but when I started to scold him, he took me by the hand, led me up to his box and left me there while he retreated to the safety of the end of his chain, and stood watching me anxiously.

I realized there must be something inside, of which he was frightened, and when I cautiously investigated I found a very small snake coiled up in the centre of his bed. After I had captured it, I found that it was a harmless type; Cholmondely, of course, could not tell the difference, and he was taking no chances.

Cholmondely was so quick at learning tricks and so willing to show off that when he returned to England, he became quite famous and even made several appearances on television, delighting the audiences by sitting on a chair, with a hat on, taking a cigarette and lighting it for himself; pouring out and drinking a glass of beer and many other things. I think he must have become rather swollen-headed with his success, for not long after this he managed to escape from the zoo and went wandering off by himself through Regent's Park, much to the horror of everyone he met. On reaching the main road, he found a bus standing there and promptly climbed aboard, for he loved being taken for a ride.

The passengers, however, decided they would rather not travel by that particular bus if Cholmondely was going to use it as well, and they were all struggling to get out when some keepers arrived from the zoo and took Cholmondely in charge. He was marched back to his cage in disgrace, but if I know Cholmondely, he must have thought it worth any amount of scoldings just for the sight of all those people trying to get off the bus together, and getting stuck in the door. Cholmondely had a great sense of humour.

Gerald Durrell
illustrated by Azoo

Scorpions in Matchboxes, Gerald!

Who is Gerald?

Aha! Don't you know who I'm talking about? Gerald Durrell — the famous Gerald Durrell! He is a lover of animals, a writer of dozens of funny tales about his real animal friends, a zoo-keeper, a maker of films about animals (haven't you seen him on TV?), a champion of animal rescue, rights and protection, an expedition leader, too.

Snails too, Gerald?

Where did all this animal business begin? Probably as soon as Gerald could crawl. His big brother Lawrence (who later became a famous writer) was complaining by 1931 that Gerald stuffed snails in his pockets and by 1935 he was stuffing scorpions in matchboxes! Ah well, when you have lived in as many different countries as young Gerald had, you could become interested in the local fauna too! Gerald Malcolm Durrell was born in India in

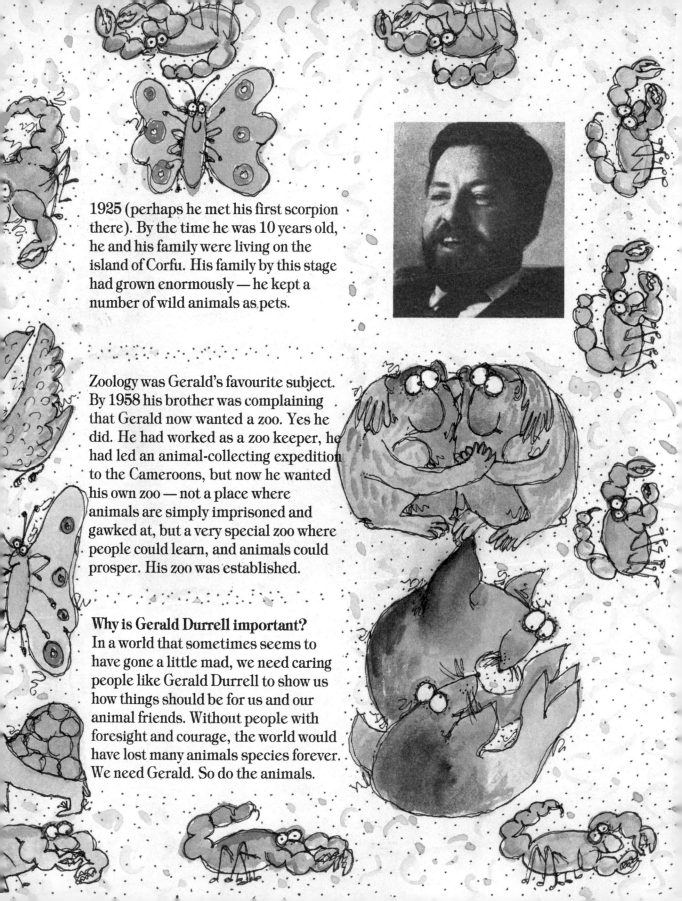

1925 (perhaps he met his first scorpion there). By the time he was 10 years old, he and his family were living on the island of Corfu. His family by this stage had grown enormously — he kept a number of wild animals as pets.

Zoology was Gerald's favourite subject. By 1958 his brother was complaining that Gerald now wanted a zoo. Yes he did. He had worked as a zoo keeper, he had led an animal-collecting expedition to the Cameroons, but now he wanted his own zoo — not a place where animals are simply imprisoned and gawked at, but a very special zoo where people could learn, and animals could prosper. His zoo was established.

Why is Gerald Durrell important?
In a world that sometimes seems to have gone a little mad, we need caring people like Gerald Durrell to show us how things should be for us and our animal friends. Without people with foresight and courage, the world would have lost many animals species forever. We need Gerald. So do the animals.

WHO ATE THE CHURCH?

A thousand miles south west of Brisbane, there's a small country town called Thargomindah. The farming folk run sheep and cattle and there are some big stations around with names like Bulloo Downs and Nockatunga.

It's not the kind of town you'd expect something weird to happen — but in 1908 something did. You see, as well as sheep and cattle, Thargomindah had lots and lots of goats. Now, there are many stories around about goats and their appetites — they're often accused of eating shirts off clothes lines, tin cans, bottles — even sticks of dynamite.

But who ever heard of goats eating a church?

Yet that's what the goats of Thargomindah did.

They ate the town's Methodist Church. Apparently it had been built with thatched-grass walls and one night the goats just started munching.

Perhaps all the hymn singing had given the walls an extra special flavour, but anyway they steadily ate away until the church was demolished.

What raised a few eyebrows was the knowledge that in lore and legend the goat is always associated with the idea of sin and with worship of the devil. People often firmly believed that the Devil, not God, created the goat, and that that's why it's such a destructive animal. Maybe old Nick had taken a hand in the whole business. I mean — imagine it. Goats eating a church!

Stories like this get my goat!

AND THE ORGAN

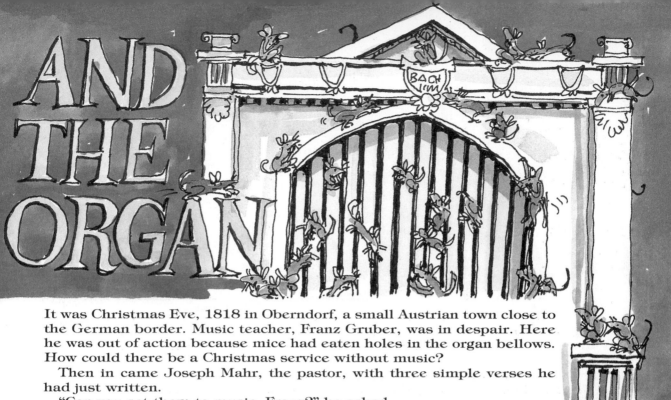

It was Christmas Eve, 1818 in Oberndorf, a small Austrian town close to the German border. Music teacher, Franz Gruber, was in despair. Here he was out of action because mice had eaten holes in the organ bellows. How could there be a Christmas service without music?

Then in came Joseph Mahr, the pastor, with three simple verses he had just written.

"Can you set them to music, Franz?" he asked.

Franz looked over the words, a tune beginning to form in his head even as he read them.

"Why, yes," he answered slowly, "but how can we manage without the organ?"

"We can sing, can't we?" said Joseph confidently, "and what about your guitar?"

Franz went to work and that night the Christmas carol "Silent Night, Holy Night" was sung for the first time at midnight mass with Joseph taking the tenor part and Franz singing bass and accompanying on the guitar.

Though they did not publish the carol, its charm was so great it was soon known throughout Austria and Germany. And people began crediting its composition to Johann Michael Haydn, younger brother of Franz Joseph Haydn. Finally in 1854, thirty-six years after that memorable Christmas, Franz (who was now choir leader and organist in the Austrian town of Hallein) spoke up and explained how the carol had been written.

In 1937, people from all over the world sent money so that a memorial chapel could be built in Oberndorf. In it are stained glass windows commemorating the men who created the world's best loved Christmas carol.

All is quiet, all is still.

Sir Gawain and the Green Knight

As it was New Year's day King Arthur held a feast at Camelot for the knights of the Round Table and the most beautiful ladies of the court.

When all were seated in the Great Hall of the castle, King Arthur rose to his feet and said "As has been my custom for many years I command none of you to touch this great feast until I have been told of some knight's glorious deed or until I have learnt of some difficult quest on which to send one of my knights." The laughter and the chatter faded away as the knights and their ladies waited to hear some great tale. Even the music stopped. But silence hung heavily in the hall. King Arthur drummed his fingers impatiently as no one rose to his command. He was just about to repeat it and chide his knights when suddenly the Great Hall doors burst open and a great gale of wind swept over them. Before them stood a strange and terrible figure.

He was a man so huge that his head almost touched the roof as he sat tall in the saddle of an enormous horse. But it was not their great size that made King Arthur and his guests gasp but the fact that the knight and his horse were green all over. Not only was he dressed in green from head to foot, but his hair, beard and skin were also the colour of new grass. The horse was a vivid green too; its green tail flicked from side to side like willow leaves in the breeze.

The knight carried no sword or shield but held aloft a huge green axe. He looked round at all the guests and cried in a voice that shook the pillars of the hall.

"Who is in charge of these weaklings?"

"I am King Arthur," said the astonished king.

"King Arthur?" said the Knight scornfully. "I see only a young boy and these others are children I could fell with one blow of my axe. Are these the famous knights of the Round Table?" He laughed and his laughter shook the room.

"Any one of these knights will answer a challenge if you care to make one," replied the king. More laughter gurgled deep within the Green Knight so that his body shook. "I will test your courage," he said. "I will give this axe to any man here and let him strike me with it while I stand without defending myself, if he will let me return the blow in a year and a day from now."

Silence hung once more in the hall. The knights all sat staring at this terrible man. The Green Knight laughed once more so that the dishes jumped on the tables. "You are not knights of the Round Table. You are cowards of the Round Table," he said.

"By heaven," said King Arthur, jumping to his feet. "I will strike your foolish head from your shoulders myself."

But Sir Gawain, King Arthur's nephew, was on his feet too. "No, let me, uncle, for I have not yet proved my worth as a knight of the Round Table."

King Arthur gasped. He was fond of his nephew but he could not refuse this request.

"At least there is one man among you," thundered the Green Knight. He immediately knelt down and put his head on the floor. Sir Gawain grasped the heavy axe and swung it with all his might. It whistled through the air. The sharp blade cut clean through the flesh and bone of the Green Knight's neck and struck the stone floor bringing up sparks from the flints. The giant green head rolled across the floor.

But the knight's body did not topple over. Instead it got up, picked up its head, mounted its horse and holding the head by the green hair, said: "Keep your side of the bargain. Seek for the knight of the Green Chapel — in the forest of the Wirral you will find it." The great horse reared and turned and with a clattering of iron hooves the Green Knight was gone.

The year went by. When the leaves began to fall from the trees Gawain knew he must set out on his quest. The court turned out to see him off. King Arthur bade him "Farewell" and then he set out northwards into the unknown. He crossed steep mountains and fierce running rivers. A dragon sprang at him from a cave and fought with him for three hours. He had to use all his strength to kill it. Then wolves chased him in a deep forest. But his wonderful horse, Gringalet, saved him. Next he battled with dwarfs who swarmed out of the craggy mountains like ants. Then an enormous bull attacked him, followed by bears and wild boars. But he fought them all off, even a tribe of ugly-looking giants that pursued him over a mountain. After all these dangers the weather now turned sharply cold. It was Christmas Eve and he imagined the comfort of the log fire at Camelot. The snow began to fall and he had no choice but to ford an icy stream to reach the land of the Wirral. Suddenly he came upon a great fence guarding a magnificent castle. He knocked hard at the gate. A porter came and let him in. He was immediately met by a large man with a great rusty-coloured beard who welcomed him to his castle.

"I seek the Green Chapel," said Sir Gawain. "I must be there by New Year's Day."

"It is yet but Christmas Eve," said the ruddy-faced man. "Rest awhile and join us in a great feast." They dressed Gawain in fine clothes and the next three days followed in feasting. The following day the lord of the castle came to him.

"I must be on my way to the Green Chapel," said Gawain.

"You are much too tired," said the red-bearded man. "You must rest for three more days. But during that time I must go hunting. As this is a merry time, let us make a joyful bargain between us. Anything I gain during my day's hunting I will give to you, but I will expect anything you gain here in the castle to be given in return to me." Gawin thought this odd but he agreed. And the lord departed at once with all his men.

Now the lady of the castle, who was extremely beautiful, had fallen in love with Gawain as soon as she saw him ride over the drawbridge. Learning that she was to be left alone in the castle with him she went at once to his room and charmed him with her talk. But Gawain, a true knight, brushed off her words of love because she was the wife of his host. But the lady was cunning and determined to have one kiss from Sir Gawain. She said to him "I do not really believe you are Sir Gawain. He would not stay for so long with one lady without giving her one kiss."

Before he could stop her she bent forward and kissed him firmly on the lips.

That night the lord came home from his hunting. He immediately presented Gawain with a deer he had caught on the hunt. Sir Gawain kissed him on the cheek.

"What have you gained during the day?" asked the lord.

"I have already given you all that I have gained," said Gawain. The lord laughed a merry laugh.

On the second day the lady again entered Sir Gawain's room and once more spoke to him of love. He still held back but she gave him two kisses before she departed. That night the lord of the castle returned carrying an enormous boar's head, which he presented to Gawain. Gawain gave him two kisses on the cheek.

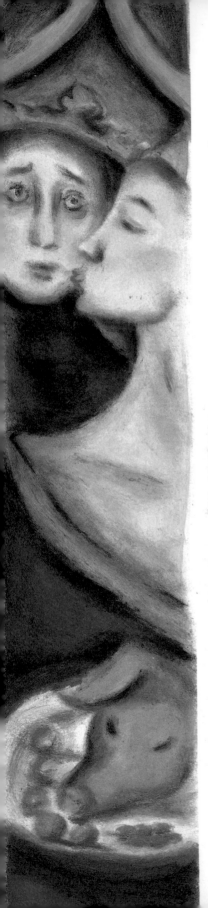

"What have you gained during the day?" asked the lord.

"I have already given you all that I have gained," said Gawain. The lord laughed a merry laugh.

On the third day the lady again entered Sir Gawain's room and spoke to him more earnestly of her love. But he did not yield though she gave him three kisses at her departure. She also gave him a gold-hemmed girdle which she said would protect him from the dangers that lay ahead in the Green Chapel. Gawain hid it under his clothes.

That night the lord again returned from his hunting and presented Gawain with the fox pelt. Gawain gave him three kisses on the cheek.

"What have you gained during the day?" asked the lord.

"I have already given you all that I have gained," said Gawain. The lord laughed a merry laugh.

Next day Gawain set off. He was surprised almost immediately to come to a chapel covered in grass, bushes and trees. The door was opened and from the inside he could hear the sound of an axe being sharpened. Trembling he dismounted from Gringalet.

"Where are you, Green Knight? I am Sir Gawain and have come to keep my part of the bargain," he called.

"I will not keep you waiting long," boomed a voice from inside. Then suddenly the Green Knight burst through the side of the Chapel, looking as large and as terrible as ever with his green hair and beard. Gawain immediately bent his head ready for the blow. The Green Knight raised the axe and then swung it down. But Gawain flinched as it whistled through the air and the Green Knight stopped it just above his neck. "You are afraid," he said. "I did not tremble when you struck off my head."

"I won't tremble again," said Gawain. "Now be quick and finish this business." Once more the knight swung the axe. It swished down. But the Green Knight's great strength stopped it just short, on the hairs of Sir Gawain's neck. Sir Gawain had not moved a centimetre.

"Now indeed I see you are a brave man," said the Knight. "This time I will strike harder."

"Hurry up!" said Gawain. "Or are you afraid to strike a defenceless man?"

For the third time the Green Knight raised his axe and hurtled it down towards Sir Gawain's waiting neck. The axe touched it but nicked only a small piece of flesh away.

"There, I have done," said the Green Knight.

Sir Gawain sprang up. He was amazed to see that the Green Knight had turned into the red-bearded lord of the castle.

"I asked my wife to tempt your knightly chivalry. You were honest with me three times, except for my wife's girdle. I have repaid you for that with that graze to your neck."

Blushing, Sir Gawain said "I will return it to you now."

"No," said the Knight. "Keep it. It will protect you from the dangers that you will face on your return journey. King Arthur's knights are indeed brave and chivalrous and merit the tales that are told of them."

Written by Paul Groves and Nigel Grimshaw
Illustrated by Rosemary Woods

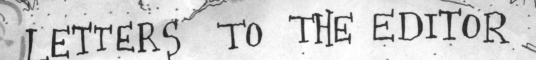

LETTERS TO THE EDITOR

2 March
Love's Young Dream Goes Sour

SIR: I am writing in protest against the views advocated in your recent article titled *Don't opt for a career, girls—wait for Prince Charming*. Apart from the stupidity of the suggestion that a career is somehow incompatible with marriage, the idea that a fairy tale romance is what every girl should aim for is not only old-fashioned, it's something that should be examined under the Trade Practices Act. Speaking as one who married the original Prince Charming, let me tell you, I'd have been far better off with a job and a decent pension to look forward to. Charming is now bald, bandy and boring. He has always been so hipped on Royal Balls that we've had one every month since we returned to the palace from our honeymoon. Imagine being sentenced to 528 Balls? And not get paid overtime? I have to watch him prancing around the floor ogling all the young things and making a complete fool of himself.

I daren't stay away for fear he falls in with some scheming young kitchen maid dressed to kill in borrowed finery and there I'll be, out on my ear without even a reference. (You'll remember I left my father's house in somewhat of a hurry.)

There ought to be compensation for losing your figure (through over-eating at banquets) and acquiring wrinkles (too many late nights), but, alas, royalty has no union. In any case, the main problem has been sheer boredom. If only I'd had a mother to point out to me that one night's dancing with a minimum of conversation is hardly the ideal courtship. Many a weary night, as I've listened to his royal snores, I've wished that silly glass slipper had fitted one of my stepsisters.

Happily ever after? What sexist rubbish!

Cinderella R
Royal Palace
Charmingville

4 March
Nocturnal Nightmares

SIR: On behalf of all occasional snorers, I protest! Queen Cinderella should try being married to someone with skin so sensitive she can even feel a pea beneath 100 mattresses. Marrying a true princess was the worst advice my mother ever gave me. Our nights are made hideous by my wife's tossing and turning and endless complaints of crumbs and wrinkles in the sheet and folds in the mattress. After a couple of hours trying to shut out the long-suffering sighs and constant remaking of the bed, I drop off only to be prodded awake after five minutes and told my snoring is keeping her awake!

Fairytale romance? Don't make me laugh!

A Prince Esq.
Nodding Castle
Kingstown

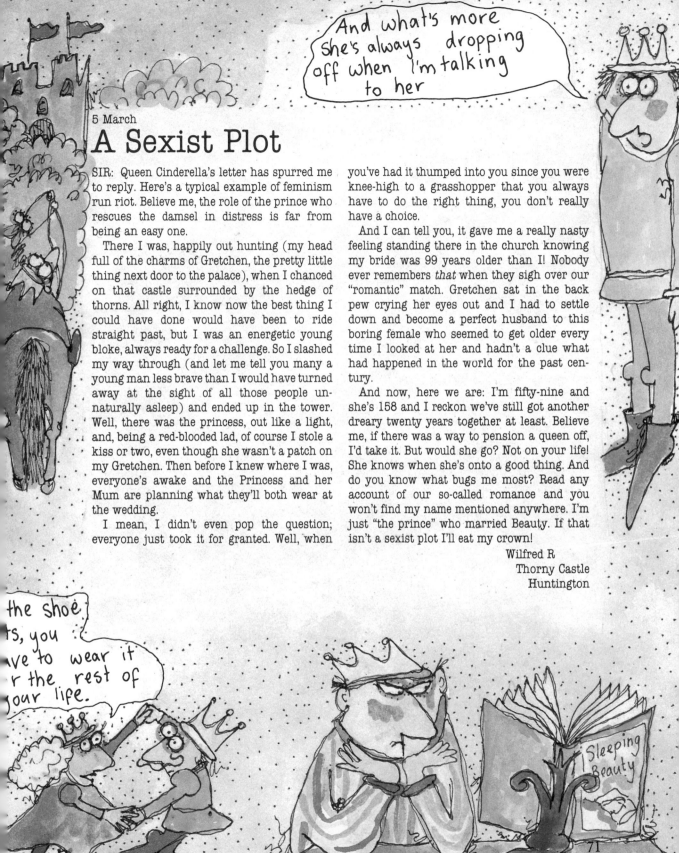

A Sexist Plot

5 March

SIR: Queen Cinderella's letter has spurred me to reply. Here's a typical example of feminism run riot. Believe me, the role of the prince who rescues the damsel in distress is far from being an easy one.

There I was, happily out hunting (my head full of the charms of Gretchen, the pretty little thing next door to the palace), when I chanced on that castle surrounded by the hedge of thorns. All right, I know now the best thing I could have done would have been to ride straight past, but I was an energetic young bloke, always ready for a challenge. So I slashed my way through (and let me tell you many a young man less brave than I would have turned away at the sight of all those people unnaturally asleep) and ended up in the tower. Well, there was the princess, out like a light, and, being a red-blooded lad, of course I stole a kiss or two, even though she wasn't a patch on my Gretchen. Then before I knew where I was, everyone's awake and the Princess and her Mum are planning what they'll both wear at the wedding.

I mean, I didn't even pop the question; everyone just took it for granted. Well, when you've had it thumped into you since you were knee-high to a grasshopper that you always have to do the right thing, you don't really have a choice.

And I can tell you, it gave me a really nasty feeling standing there in the church knowing my bride was 99 years older than I! Nobody ever remembers *that* when they sigh over our "romantic" match. Gretchen sat in the back pew crying her eyes out and I had to settle down and become a perfect husband to this boring female who seemed to get older every time I looked at her and hadn't a clue what had happened in the world for the past century.

And now, here we are: I'm fifty-nine and she's 158 and I reckon we've still got another dreary twenty years together at least. Believe me, if there was a way to pension a queen off, I'd take it. But would she go? Not on your life! She knows when she's onto a good thing. And do you know what bugs me most? Read any account of our so-called romance and you won't find my name mentioned anywhere. I'm just "the prince" who married Beauty. If that isn't a sexist plot I'll eat my crown!

Wilfred R
Thorny Castle
Huntington

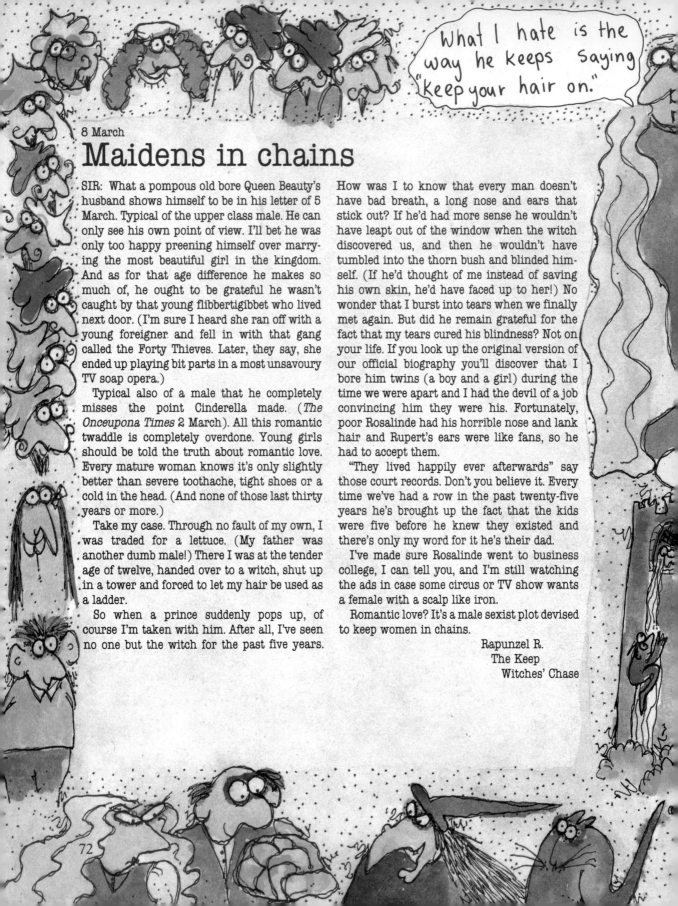

What I hate is the way he keeps saying "keep your hair on."

8 March

Maidens in chains

SIR: What a pompous old bore Queen Beauty's husband shows himself to be in his letter of 5 March. Typical of the upper class male. He can only see his own point of view. I'll bet he was only too happy preening himself over marrying the most beautiful girl in the kingdom. And as for that age difference he makes so much of, he ought to be grateful he wasn't caught by that young flibbertigibbet who lived next door. (I'm sure I heard she ran off with a young foreigner and fell in with that gang called the Forty Thieves. Later, they say, she ended up playing bit parts in a most unsavoury TV soap opera.)

Typical also of a male that he completely misses the point Cinderella made. (*The Onceupona Times* 2 March). All this romantic twaddle is completely overdone. Young girls should be told the truth about romantic love. Every mature woman knows it's only slightly better than severe toothache, tight shoes or a cold in the head. (And none of those last thirty years or more.)

Take my case. Through no fault of my own, I was traded for a lettuce. (My father was another dumb male!) There I was at the tender age of twelve, handed over to a witch, shut up in a tower and forced to let my hair be used as a ladder.

So when a prince suddenly pops up, of course I'm taken with him. After all, I've seen no one but the witch for the past five years.

How was I to know that every man doesn't have bad breath, a long nose and ears that stick out? If he'd had more sense he wouldn't have leapt out of the window when the witch discovered us, and then he wouldn't have tumbled into the thorn bush and blinded himself. (If he'd thought of me instead of saving his own skin, he'd have faced up to her!) No wonder that I burst into tears when we finally met again. But did he remain grateful for the fact that my tears cured his blindness? Not on your life. If you look up the original version of our official biography you'll discover that I bore him twins (a boy and a girl) during the time we were apart and I had the devil of a job convincing him they were his. Fortunately, poor Rosalinde had his horrible nose and lank hair and Rupert's ears were like fans, so he had to accept them.

"They lived happily ever afterwards" say those court records. Don't you believe it. Every time we've had a row in the past twenty-five years he's brought up the fact that the kids were five before he knew they existed and there's only my word for it he's their dad.

I've made sure Rosalinde went to business college, I can tell you, and I'm still watching the ads in case some circus or TV show wants a female with a scalp like iron.

Romantic love? It's a male sexist plot devised to keep women in chains.

Rapunzel R.
The Keep
Witches' Chase

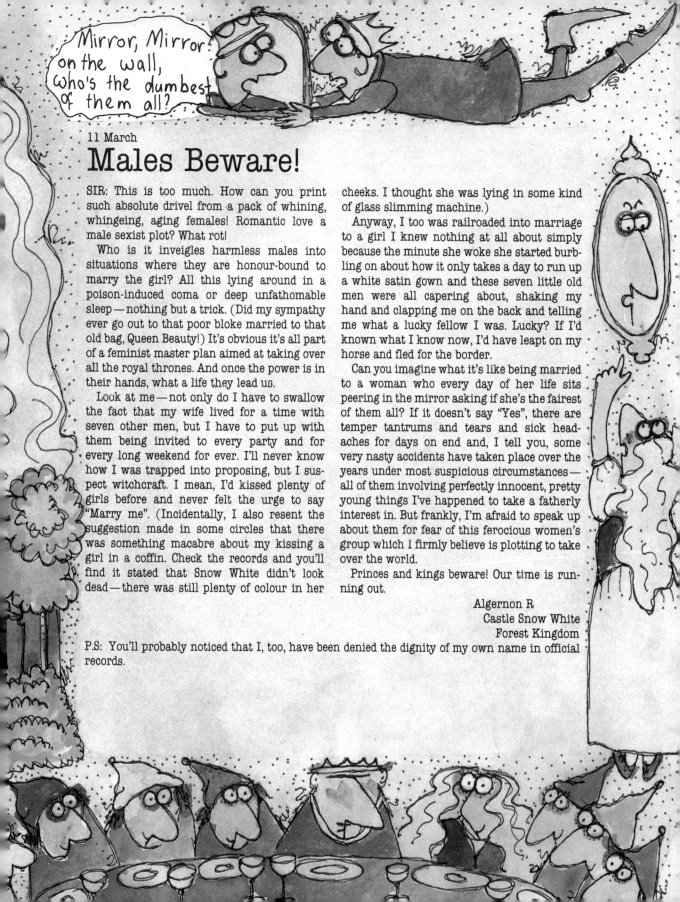

Mirror, Mirror on the wall, who's the dumbest of them all?

Males Beware!

SIR: This is too much. How can you print such absolute drivel from a pack of whining, whingeing, aging females! Romantic love a male sexist plot? What rot!

Who is it inveigles harmless males into situations where they are honour-bound to marry the girl? All this lying around in a poison-induced coma or deep unfathomable sleep—nothing but a trick. (Did my sympathy ever go out to that poor bloke married to that old bag, Queen Beauty!) It's obvious it's all part of a feminist master plan aimed at taking over all the royal thrones. And once the power is in their hands, what a life they lead us.

Look at me—not only do I have to swallow the fact that my wife lived for a time with seven other men, but I have to put up with them being invited to every party and for every long weekend for ever. I'll never know how I was trapped into proposing, but I suspect witchcraft. I mean, I'd kissed plenty of girls before and never felt the urge to say "Marry me". (Incidentally, I also resent the suggestion made in some circles that there was something macabre about my kissing a girl in a coffin. Check the records and you'll find it stated that Snow White didn't look dead—there was still plenty of colour in her cheeks. I thought she was lying in some kind of glass slimming machine.)

Anyway, I too was railroaded into marriage to a girl I knew nothing at all about simply because the minute she woke she started burbling on about how it only takes a day to run up a white satin gown and these seven little old men were all capering about, shaking my hand and clapping me on the back and telling me what a lucky fellow I was. Lucky? If I'd known what I know now, I'd have leapt on my horse and fled for the border.

Can you imagine what it's like being married to a woman who every day of her life sits peering in the mirror asking if she's the fairest of them all? If it doesn't say "Yes", there are temper tantrums and tears and sick headaches for days on end and, I tell you, some very nasty accidents have taken place over the years under most suspicious circumstances—all of them involving perfectly innocent, pretty young things I've happened to take a fatherly interest in. But frankly, I'm afraid to speak up about them for fear of this ferocious women's group which I firmly believe is plotting to take over the world.

Princes and kings beware! Our time is running out.

Algernon R
Castle Snow White
Forest Kingdom

P.S: You'll probably noticed that I, too, have been denied the dignity of my own name in official records.

13 March
It's a Man's World!

SIR: I am surprised and alarmed that such a reputable paper as *The Onceupona Times* will allow so much space for the ravings of a couple of weak-kneed, lily-livered male chauvinists. I pity their poor wives, although I believe that this so-called fairytale romance myth has served me worst of all.

Not only is my sixty-year old husband grossly overweight (he takes up at least three-quarters of our marriage bed even though it's, naturally, a king-sized one), he also has the most alarming bulbous eyes and spends an appalling length of time each day in the bath.

And how would you like trying to explain to six children that their father was once a frog?

Now it turns out that one of our grand-children has webbed feet, while another croaks alarmingly whenever she gets near a pond or swamp.

Imagine the dreadful life I've lived (how could I invite my in-laws to anything?) and then try to talk to me of sexist plots. Ah, if only I'd been allowed to take up a career playing professional netball or lawn bowls, how happy I would be now.

Believe me, it's a man's and a frog's world!

Mary Anne R
Amphibia Palace
Aqueausville

P.S. Ever noticed how he gets top billing in our story?

16 March
A Beastly Tale

SIR: This is a plea for all unmarried girls to take to heart the sad stories of those of us who fell for the line that all a girl had to do was be beautiful, good and dutiful and she'd catch herself a prince. I too was conned. I married a Beast and he stayed a beast. And all because I was trapped first by pity for my father, then for the man who tricked me into marrying

him. Dying of unrequited love, indeed! Believe me, he made a miraculous recovery the moment the knot was tied.

He has driven me mad with his penny-pinching, his bad temper and his habit of pretending he is mortally ill whenever he can't get his own way.

I should have known, once a beast—always a beast!

Name and address supplied but withheld at request of writer.

Nothing but codswallop?

SIR: I am staggered by the recent correspondence on the topic of fairytale romance. A bigger load of codswallop I can't imagine.

There's only one way to deal with an unsatisfactory marriage and that's to end it swiftly and finally. It's a remedy that never

fails, especially as there are always plenty of willing young things out there ready to do anything to get a plain gold band on that third finger, left hand.

Don't muck about. Finish things off, that's my advice.

G ("Blue") Beard
Doomsday Hall
Dangerville

18 March

A Boy's Best Friend...

SIR: Just a line or two to say that the letters about fairytale romance have made me realise how lucky I have been to escape it. Despite rumours to the contrary I did not marry a princess. I stayed on with my dear old Mum (whose sharp tongue sweetened up considerably once I brought home the gold) and that dear little golden-egg-laying hen. A sweeter creature you could never meet. She had the most beautiful feathers and her gentle cluck, cluck when she perched on my knee every night was music to my ears—better than anything that useless golden harp produced.

After Mum died, Henny Penny and I lived happily ever after until, alas, she passed away. Now I sit alone dreaming of those happy hours we spent together.

My advice to all you princes out there is to save your money and get a nice pet.

Jack Farmer
Beanstalk Cottage
Pastoral Land

Editor's note: It seems appropriate at this point to declare this correspondence now closed.
Pat Edwards

Little Red Riding Hood and the Wolf

As soon as Wolf began to feel
That he would like a decent meal,
He went and knocked on Grandma's door.
When Grandma opened it, she saw
The sharp white teeth, the horrid grin,
And Wolfie said, "May I come in?"
Poor Grandmamma was terrified,
"He's going to eat me up!" she cried.

And she was absolutely right.
He ate her up in one big bite.
But Grandmamma was small and tough,
And Wolfie wailed, "That's not enough!
"I haven't yet begun to feel
"That I have had a decent meal!"
He ran around the kitchen yelping,
"I've *got* to have another helping!"
Then added with a frightful leer,
"I'm therefore going to wait right here
"Till Little Miss Red Riding Hood · ·
"Comes home from walking in the wood."
He quickly put on Grandma's clothes,
(Of course he hadn't eaten those.)

He dressed himself in coat and hat.
He put on shoes and after that
He even brushed and curled his hair,
Then sat himself in Grandma's chair.
In came the little girl in red.
She stopped. She stared. And then she said,
"*What great big ears you have, Grandma.*"
"*All the better to hear you with,*" the Wolf replied.
"*What great big eyes you have, Grandma,*"
said Little Red Riding Hood.
"*All the better to see you with,*" the Wolf replied.

He sat there watching her and smiled.
He thought, I'm going to eat this child.
Compared with her old Grandmamma
She's going to taste like caviare.

Then Little Red Riding Hood said, "*But Grandma,
what a lovely great big furry coat you have on.*"

"That's wrong!" cried Wolf, "Have you forgot
"To tell me what BIG TEETH I've got?
"Ah well, no matter what you say,
"I'm going to eat you anyway."
The small girl smiles. One eyelid flickers.
She whips a pistol from her knickers.
She aims it at the creature's head
And *bang bang bang*, she shoots him dead.

A few weeks later, in the wood,
I came across Miss Riding Hood.
But what a change! No cloak of red,
No silly hood upon her head.
She said, "Hello, and do please note
"My lovely furry WOLFSKIN COAT."

by Roald Dahl
illustrated by Quentin Blake

THE LADY OR THE TIGER

Faced with an impossible choice? Agonising over which decision you'll make when either course could lead to disaster? That's when an older person just might say "Guess it's a case of the lady or the tiger!"

A funny comment? Not if you've heard the classic story of that name. It was written by American author Francis Stockton and published in 1884. Its cliffhanger ending created a sensation at the time and earned the writer a reputation that has lasted long after all his other books had been forgotten. What's so novel about it? Read it for yourself—and see.

Once, in a far-off barbaric kingdom, there lived a beautiful princess. She was wilful and spoilt, for her every wish had been granted since childhood. She was also passionate and cruel.

Now the princess took a lover without her father's knowledge or permission and when the king found out he ordered that the young man should be arrested immediately. The sentence passed down was that he must appear in a public arena and there, in front of the princess and the whole court, open one of two doors. Behind one, he is told, waits a ferocious tiger that will immediately tear him to pieces. Behind the other, is a lovely maiden whom he must straightway wed. He has also learned secretly that the princess has discovered the secret of the doors and will signal to him which he should open. But alas, our hero remembers only too well how jealous his princess is, how often she has told him that she would sooner see him dead than in the arms of another.

Nevertheless, he turns to her as he stands alone in the arena. With a gesture, the princess directs him to one of the doors. He strides towards it and flings it open.

And here the story ends …

WHICH CAME OUT OF THE OPENED DOOR—THE LADY OR THE TIGER?

THE PROBLEM	THE SOLUTION	
1 People's eyes aren't always as good as they'd like them to be—especially as they get older.	SPECTACLES (or glasses as we often call them)	
2 Some bright spark way back had discovered that the gum that oozed from certain trees was good to chew, but it lost its strength and taste pretty fast. They needed something better.	CHEWING GUM	
3 Everyone who drank too much wanted a tonic that would cure a morning-after hangover.	COCA COLA	
4 Those ring-pull tabs on cans of soft-drink and beer often broke and added to pollution.	POP-TOP CANS	
5 In 1848 a 20 year old American named Levi Strauss had done pretty well on the California gold fields. He'd sold all the bales of cloth he'd bought in New York to the miners— except a roll of canvas he'd thought might be used for patching tents. And he needed that cash to get a good stake on the diggings.	JEANS	
6 Mary Anderson of Birmingham, Alabama, loved travelling on New York's electric trolleys when she visited there in 1902, but she got nervous when it rained. Mary noticed the driver could hardly see out of the wind-screen in bad weather.	WINDSCREEN WIPERS	

THE SOLVER

We don't know his name. We do know that he was Italian and lived in Pisa around 1286. Almost certainly he was a craftsman working with glass. The first spectacles were made only for far-sighted people. It wasn't until the late 15th century that concave lenses for the short-sighted were developed. And it was good old Ben Franklin (of kite-flying fame) who came up with the idea of bi-focals. (His problem? Constantly having to change from one pair of specs to another.)

Some books say US forest-worker, John B. Curtis, others say it was another American, Thomas Adams Jnr. Tom's problem was that his attempt to make rubber out of chicle (or gum) from the sapodilla tree had been a flop. So what did he do? He added some sugar and flavour and invented chewing gum. Where does the name Wrigley come into it? Ah, Will Wrigley also had a problem. Sales were down in his father's baking-powder factory, so Will decided to give away packets of this new chewing gum with every order he got from grocers. The gum proved more popular than the baking powder, so Will set up a chewing gum factory. In no time the world was chomping on Spearmint, Juicy Fruit and PK, and Will was a millionaire.

Old Dr Pemberton of Atlanta, Georgia, was a whiz at running up patent medicines to soothe American folks' nerves, so one day he decided to try to make one that would cure a hangover and pep people up. A friend in a drug store with a soda fountain agreed to test it on customers. After a few trials and errors — lo and behold, coca cola was born! By 1974, 88 years after its invention, over 165 million cokes a day were being downed in 135 different countries — but to cure a thirst, not a hangover.

In 1973, Mike Debenham of Victoria, Australia, came up with a bright idea. Why not push a hole in the can so the circle of metal falls inside? He showed his invention on *The Inventors* TV Show and won the award for the best invention of the year. BHP and Comalco developed the idea and Mike's cans were soon popping up (or rather in) all over the world.

Levi noticed that miners' pants wore out very quickly. "Why not make the canvas into trousers?" he thought. They sold like hot cakes even though the material was so tough he had to use copper rivets in places instead of just stitching. Before long Levi was in business — not as a golddigger but as a manufacturer of canvas trousers (which he called Levis) for miners and cowboys. But Levi had struck gold all right. His pants were to become the world's most popular article of clothing.

Once home, Mary decided she could come up with a solution. She attached a handle to a rubber blade so that a driver could turn the handle back and forth to wipe off rain and snow. Critics fell about, laughing at Mary's silly window cleaning device, but drivers loved it. Now no-one can imagine driving without them.

CONFLICT

Fourteen year old Derin's world is a troubled one, full of strange problems. It is a land in which there have always been two leaders—a King who rules over the Council at Iri-Nan, and one called the Warden of the Grove, head of the Sacred Circle. For generations these leaders had warred, setting the people of the plains against those of the uplands and mountains. Peace had come in Derin's grandparents' time, thanks to a great leader named Wenborn the Wise, but lately things have gone wrong. The Iri-Nan Council has sent soldiers to the uplands to capture farmers to use in their army, and many young folk have run off to offer their support to the Sacred Circle of the Grove.

Derin's father is one of those taken by the soldiers and now Derin and Marna, his childhood nurse, are searching for him, desperately hoping they can help the older man escape. But the going is hard. Derin is a cripple, lame from birth, forced to use a crutch. Marna is old and the ground is slippery, for the heavy winter snows are only just melting into slush and mud. And they are moving through a countryside in which people are suspicious of strangers, one in which the name 'Witch' no longer means Wise person, but rather someone to be feared, someone to be killed.

On the day before, much had happened. Derin, who has always had an attraction for animals, had been adopted by a large black raven. He has named it Craak. At night, at Sone village inn, they had met a strange traveller, one with blank unseeing eyes, like eyes of the dead. There had also been an encounter with a belligerent soldier who accused them of being Witch people. Marna managed to confuse him until they could escape, but they start the morning knowing they have made an enemy.

The second day passed in much the same way as the first, except that by late afternoon they had again reached a more wooded area, the rolling upland country dotted regularly with small groups of trees. That night, as they were sitting before the camp fire, Derin said:

"Surely the woodlands must be quite close by now. When do you think we'll get there?"

Marna was already dozing fitfully, but she jerked awake in response to his question.

"Provided we don't waste too much time in Solwyck," she replied, "we should reach the outer limits of the woodlands by tomorrow afternoon."

"Solwyck?" he said, surprised. "But that's a village. Why are we going there?"

Marna held both hands out, as if to show him how empty they were.

"We've finished the bread," she explained, "and Solwyck is only a few miles from here. We must go there first in order to collect more food."

"But won't it be dangerous?" he objected. "Wouldn't it be safer in the cover of the woodlands?"

She sighed impatiently.

"Use your brains, child," she said. "What earthly good is safety to us if we're starving? In any case, haven't you realized yet that this whole journey is dangerous? Or is that perhaps what disturbs you?"

He didn't answer. And seeing the hurt and worried expression on his face, she relented and added:

"It needn't be too dangerous, not if we're careful. We can leave Craak outside the village and I can pretend I'm a blind beggar." She held up the tattered edges of her cloak and laughed. "At least I'll look the part. With you leading me, I'll appear so old and helpless that no one will give us a second glance."

And that was precisely what they did. The next morning, an hour or two after sunrise, they left Craak in a huge oak tree that grew beside the road and walked slowly into the village.

As Marna had predicted, they excited no interest in the few passers-by. With Derin holding her hand and Marna shuffling along beside him, her eyes closed and back bent almost double, they were exactly like a blind beggar and her guide; and they reached the centre of the village without once being challenged.

Solwyck was a much bigger place than Sone. The main street was quite wide and strewn with gravel; and in addition to several small shops, it boasted no fewer than three taverns. The most popular of the three was an ugly two-storey building made of wood and roughly cut stone; and outside it, on benches placed along the southern wall, was gathered a group of old men and women obviously enjoying the early spring sunshine.

Marna took in the scene through narrowly opened eyes and murmured softly to Derin:

"We'll stop here. Nobody will notice me amongst so many old people."

He led her over to an empty space on one of the benches and helped her sit down. Further along the bench an old man with a bald head and a broad, very red face leaned towards her and said in a friendly way:

"Good morning to you, mother. Isn't it good to feel the warm spring sunshine on your face again?"

Instead of answering, she cackled foolishly and rolled her eyes upwards.

"What was that? What was that?" she said in a quavery voice, cupping one hand around her ear.

Derin bent forward and shouted:

"The man's talking to you, Gran. He says he's enjoying the sunshine."

"Ah, the spring, the spring," she said, wiping her eyes with the tips of her fingers as though she were crying. "I didn't think to survive another season. Not with everyone deserting their homes or dying. I kept thinking, I'll be the next one to go. And I will be, too, you'll see."

"Don't take on, mother," the red-faced man bawled at her. "With luck, there're quite a few years left in us yet."

Marna, her sadness vanishing as quickly as it had appeared, cackled foolishly once again.

"He talks about years," she quavered. "I've forgotten about years. One day at a time is what I say, one day at a time."

As she spoke, she plucked at her cloak, in the manner of one who no longer has anything useful to do with her hands. And even Derin, who knew she was acting, was almost convinced by her transformation.

"Can I get you something to eat, Gran?" he shouted.

"Ah, food and drink," she mumbled, "food and drink. That's all there is left. That and a little sleep."

With shaking hands she fumbled inside her cloak and pulled out a cloth purse. From this, working only by touch, she selected some copper coins and placed them in Derin's palm.

"See what you can get us," she said, "and don't let them cheat you. I'll soon be gone from this world, and then you'll have to fend for yourself."

Leaving her sitting on the bench, he limped into the tavern. A hard-faced woman was standing behind the counter. She was a typical uplander: strongly built, with light brown hair and grey eyes.

"You're a stranger in these parts," she said suspiciously.

"We're beggar folk," he explained. "I travel with my grandmother, who's blind."

The woman nodded, accepting his story but obviously unmoved by it.

"These are difficult times for everyone," she said defensively. "There's barely enough food to go round, and we're certainly in no position to give charity, not even to beggar folk."

Derin resisted the temptation to make an angry reply.

"I have money," he said coolly, sliding the coppers across the counter towards her. "Can you give me some ale and as much food as you think they are worth?"

The woman counted the coppers slowly before dropping them into a drawer below the counter. Then she filled a small jug with ale and placed beside it several hard brown loaves and a good-sized square of cheese. With all these cradled in his left arm, Derin limped back outside.

During his brief absence nothing much seemed to have happened. One other figure, draped in a heavy cloak and hood, had joined the group of old people, but that was all. Marna was sitting exactly as he had left her: leaning back against the sun-warmed stones of the wall, eyes closed, a foolish, vacant smile on her lips.

"Here you are, Gran," he said loudly, "drink some of this and we'll be on our way."

She accepted the jug and took a long grateful drink. But as she handed it back to him, she grasped his wrist and pulled him towards her.

"Stay here a few minutes," she whispered softly, "and keep your ears open."

Reluctantly, he sat down beside her and listened.

The red-faced man who had spoken to them earlier was saying:

"I don't care what you think, it's just a passing phase. Some young hot-head in the Council at Iri-Nan has heard a few ugly rumours, he's panicked, and sent the soldiers up here. That's all there is to it, if you ask me. Give them a few more months of running round the countryside — they'll soon discover they're on a wild-goose chase — and then they'll pack up and go home."

A tiny old woman answered him. She had small, pinched features and long snow-white hair that was neatly plaited and wound tightly around her head.

"It's all very well calling it a passing phase," she said, "but can we dismiss it as easily as that? What about the talk of soldiers being killed no more than a mile from the village? And what persuaded the young men and women to run off as they have — some of them to the mountains, others to Iri-Nan?"

"Do you expect me to believe all that nonsense about soldiers dying?" the red-faced man replied. "Those are just stories they tell to win us over. They know they'd get little sympathy from us otherwise. And as for the young folk, you mark my words, they'll be back just as soon as all this nonsense blows over."

Several of the others voiced their approval of these sentiments, and it was just beginning to appear that the discussion was over when a thin, wizened old man rose shakily to his feet. He was so ancient that the flesh seemed to have shrunk away from his bones; and the bones themselves had grown thin and sharp with age, so that now he looked more like a featherless bird than a human being.

"Stuff and nonsense!" he broke out in a high, piping voice. "Stuff and nonsense, I say."

"Now don't get yourself all a-tremble," someone called out, not unkindly.

The old man glared at the speaker, as though daring him at his peril to interrupt again.

"You all know me," he said, his bird-like head trembling on his thin stalk of a neck. "And you all know how old I am. A hundred and seven years this equinox." He paused, allowing the awful fact of his age to have its sobering effect on the audience. "A hundred and seven," he repeated, "and my father nigh on a hundred before me. Between us we've seen and heard more of the goings-on in these parts than all the rest of you put together. And I'm telling you now that there's a deal more than rumours abroad. D'you want to know what I think?" Again he paused, giving his audience time to prepare themselves for what was to come. "I think the days of the old Kingdom have returned."

There were murmurs of shocked disbelief from most of his listeners. The tiny white-haired woman said:

"But Wenborn the Wise promised us that those days would never come back again."

"Aye, he promised us," the old man piped shrilly, "but did he have the power to make good that promise? That's what we have to ask ourselves. Think back, every one of you. After the long wars, what happened to the Warden's Staff? The one, we were told, that was made from the topmost branch of the oldest tree in the Grove? Fire, they say, couldn't burn it, nor any axe split it. And what about the Sword of the Kings? The one which was supposed to be older than the human race and was always kept locked up in the Citadel? Hard enough to split rocks, it was."

"They were both destroyed!" the red-faced man burst out. "Wenborn the Wise told us he destroyed them."

"That is indeed what he told us," the old man replied, his bird-like head trembling more violently than ever, "but for all his wisdom, did he have the power to carry out such a deed? Look at what's happening around us now, and then answer that question truthfully. No, the Sword and the Staff still exist. And so I tell you again, whether you like it or not, the days of the old Kingdom have returned; and all of you here" — pointing a claw-like finger at everyone present — "are destined to end your days as I began mine: with the noise of war thundering in your ears."

As he sat down there was an immediate outburst from most of the other old people, many of them shouting or talking at once. In the midst of all the confusion, Marna rose slowly to her feet.

"Come," she whispered in Derin's ear, "time for us to be leaving."

But before they could steal away, the hard-faced woman who had sold Derin the food came running out into the street.

"Stop all this noise, you old fools!" she shouted harshly. "What are you trying to do? Bring the soldiers down on us?"

No sooner had she spoken than two soldiers appeared at the far end of the street. Attracted by the shouting, they hurried down towards the tavern. To his dismay, Derin noticed that one of them was the soldier who had confronted them in the inn at Sone. Quickly he hissed a warning to Marna and they both turned away, Derin sliding his crutch round in front of him in the hope that it wouldn't be noticed.

"What's going on here?" the soldier shouted. "Be silent!"

But the old people, once roused, were not easily quelled. The wizened old man who had spoken of the return of the Kingdom rose shakily to his feet once more and screeched out:

"There they are, the ones who claim to protect us. But I've lived in the shadow of their rule before. Murderers, every one of them!"

The tall, pale-faced soldier drew his sword and pointed it at the old man's quivering neck.

"There'll be no more talk like that," he said threateningly. "And that goes for everyone here."

He ran his eye slowly over the rest of the crowd — and it was then that he spotted Derin and Marna.

"You!" he shouted triumphantly, and leaped towards them.

Derin, in spite of his lame foot, managed somehow to dodge to, one side. But Marna was not so lucky. She too tried to dodge, and in doing so stumbled and almost fell. She was given no chance to regain her footing. As she struggled to keep her balance, at the precise moment when she was most helpless, the soldier swung his arm, catching her on the side of the head with the flat of his sword and knocking her senseless to the ground.

There was a shocked silence from the rest of the crowd.

Derin, convinced that she was dead, had drawn his dagger almost without realizing what he was doing.

"You've killed her!" he said in a hoarse, tear-choked voice.

He looked helplessly at the weapon in his hand. He knew, even before he moved, that the short, rusted blade was useless against the soldier's steel sword. Yet still he leaped forward, lunging at the mailed figure before him. It was more an act of desperation than a real attempt to injure his opponent — an act, as he realized afterwards, of sadness and defeat.

The soldier, had he wanted to, could have killed him at will. Instead, he merely knocked the flimsy blade from Derin's hand.

Scrambling backwards as quickly as he could, Derin retrieved the dagger and again faced his attacker.

"Listen to me, witch boy," the soldier said, "my orders are to take you alive, and if I can, I will. But if you force me to, I'll kill you."

That brief pause had given Derin time to think. He again looked at the dagger, and with a shrug of resignation pushed it back into its scabbard. The soldier, nodding his approval, lowered his sword slightly. That was what Derin had been waiting for. In one swift movement he swung the crutch upwards and thrust the heavy metal tip straight at his opponent, catching him just below the chin. As the man staggered back, choking and clawing at his throat, Derin whirled the crutch through a full circle and brought it down on the side of his jaw, knocking him unconscious.

The watching crowd gave a murmur of approval. But Derin knew the struggle wasn't over yet: the other soldier still had to be dealt with; and unlike his companion he was completely on his guard. Already he had drawn his sword and begun inching forward.

As quickly as he could, Derin moved further out into the street in order to give himself more space, and then began whirling the crutch above his head. For days he had cursed this cumbersome piece of wood on which he had to rely, but now, at a moment of crisis, it was unaccountably light, moving easily in his hands, the metal tip flashing dangerously in the sunlight as it swung through a tight protective circle at the centre of which Derin stood secure. Never, it seemed, had he felt more confident, more sure of success, and he had actually started to advance on his opponent when he was distracted by someone groaning near by. Briefly he glanced aside, and was delighted to find Marna sitting up, holding both hands to her head.

Yet now it was Derin's turn to be caught unawares. Seizing his opportunity, the soldier charged forward. But before he could take more than a pace or two, there was a muffled thud and he faltered in his stride, a surprised expression on his face. He took two more dragging steps, there was another thud, and his sword slipped from his fingers and fell with a clatter to the gravelled roadway. The soldier now seemed to be pleading with his enemy, his mouth drawn open in a voiceless cry of anguish, his eyes wide with pain and surprise. Derin, mystified, had ceased to whirl the crutch above his head. He stood quite still as the man reached out, touching him lightly on the shoulder, before he stumbled, fell to his knees, and finally, with a soft moan, pitched forward onto the road.

For a moment or two Derin was totally confused. Then, as the first wave of astonishment passed, he saw that there were two arrows protruding from the man's back. It wasn't the first time he had seen such arrows: one identical to these had mortally wounded the soldier whom he and Marna had found lying in the snow.

Without hesitation Derin crouched down and placed his fingers on the man's neck, searching for a pulse. But there was none: he was dead. And there, twenty paces away, standing in the middle of the road, was his assailant: his heavy cloak thrown open, the bow still in his hand, the hood pulled back from his head.

Earlier, when he had emerged from the tavern and noticed this figure sitting at the end of the far bench, Derin had taken him for one of the old people. Now there was no mistaking his identity: the thick woollen muffler around the lower part of the face; the dead eyes staring at him. As on that night at the inn, Derin felt drawn by those eyes, by something hidden within them, which was trying to reach out and probe his mind; some distant force which sought to stir into wakefulness his lost memory. Slowly Derin raised his own eyes towards the muffled face; but before he could meet that dead gaze, Marna called out to him.

"Are you going to stand there all day, boy?" she said irritably. "Can't you even help an old woman get up?"

She was sitting on the ground beside the wall, and he went over and eased her to her feet. She placed both arms on his shoulders and leaned heavily against him, as though she were still dizzy. But he soon realized that it was merely a trick to get close to him.

"Whatever you do," she whispered urgently, "don't look into his eyes."

Aloud, she went on in a grumbling voice;

"I don't know what the world's coming to. You arrive at a village, looking for a bit of company, and this is the way you're treated. Here we are, innocent people who've never harmed a soul, and yet anyone can happen along and bully and beat us as they please. Well, we know when we're not wanted. Come, boy, let's get away from here. Let's leave them to their wars or their fights or whatever it is they think they're doing."

While she was grumbling on, she groped along the wooden bench and gathered up the loaves and cheese they had bought earlier, stuffing them into pockets inside her cloak. Then, watched by the astonished crowd of old people and by the sinister figure of the unknown bowman, she hooked her hand through Derin's arm, and together they hurried away down the sunlit street.

by Victor Kelleher
illustrated by Gaston Vanzet

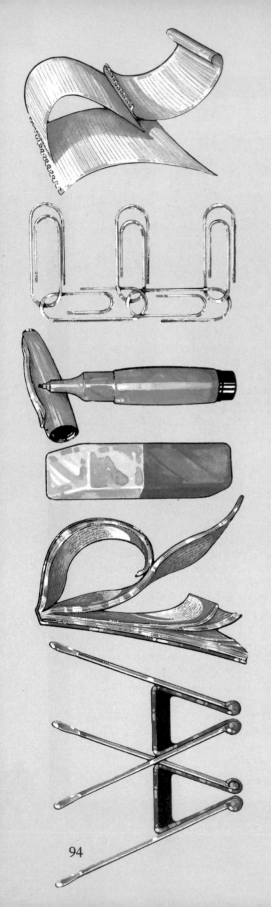

Name: _Victor Kelleher_

Born at: _London England_

Born on: _19th July, 1939_

Started school at: _Can't remember!_

Favourite subjects at school: _Morning recess_

What I didn't like about school: _The bell ringing at the start of school each day_

Favourite food when young: _Chips, toast_

Favourite food now: _Chips, avocados_

Best-loved story or book when young: _Robin Hood stories_

Favourite kind of books now: _Novels – all kinds_

Three things I love: _Hot weather, gorillas, movies_

Three things I hate: _Motor mowers, abattoirs, getting up early_

AUTHOR VICTOR KELLEHER

Secret wish: _ORF GNOL NDA PYPAH FEIL_

Favourite riddle or joke: _What do you call a man with a hundred rabbits up his nose? WARREN_

Ethnic background — parents: _Not very sure, but_

— grandparents: _Lots of Irish_

Autograph: _Victor Kelleher._

Victor Kelleher invented me!

Why did you eat it, PERSEPHONE?

Who was Persephone?

She's the one we have to thank for the fact that we don't have eternal summer, according to Greek mythology.

What was her problem?

Being too beautiful seems to be the answer to that one.

Persephone was daughter of Zeus, the supreme god, ruler of both gods and humans, and Demeter, goddess of agricultural fertility and protector of marriage and women. So lovely was she, her mother doted on her.

(Sickening, isn't it? None of these ancient beings ever seem to have been fat, pimply or short-sighted).

Enter the villain, and, like all crooks, he has an alias. He's sometimes called Hades, sometimes Pluto. And just to confuse the issue, his kingdom is also usually referred to as Hades. He's a real toughie—fierce and unyielding, a grim, terrible god, deaf to the prayers of mortals and quite contemptuous of human sacrifices. But he's also the giver of wealth or of blessings which come from the earth, so you couldn't exactly ignore him. Brother to Zeus and Poseidon, Pluto helped him when they overthrew Cronus and then claimed the lower regions, or the underworld as his kingdom. The name Hades meant "the unseen" and people shuddered at the name. In fact you could say Pluto was top of everyone's hate list. Which all adds up to a far from perfect son-in-law for Demeter.

Pluto, it seems, fell madly in love with Persephone. (They were an immoral lot and the fact that she was his niece made no difference.) Zeus agreed to their marriage, but Demeter had other ideas.

"Get lost", she told him, in suitably royal language, "my girl's not for you!".

Now Pluto wasn't one to take a brush-off, so the first chance he got he snatched her away from her flower-picking (no dreary housework or school for the immortals) and nipped off to the underworld with her.

To say Demeter was upset, is putting it mildly. She moped around the world, searching for her beloved daughter and the earth mourned with her. Trees dropped their leaves and stood bare. Flowers wilted and died, the grass turned brown, the sun no longer shone.

Fed up with all the gloom and the cold (up till now they'd had eternal summer), Zeus sent Hermes, messenger of the gods, to hunt for Persephone, and when Hermes brought back word that the girl was a prisoner in the underworld, Zeus ordered that Hermes was to hop right back there and bring the girl home. However, there was one condition. Persephone was free to come only if she had eaten no food at all while living in Hades.

But alas, Persephone had eaten part of a pomegranate. She pleaded with her dad that she had swallowed only six seeds, so he relented a little. Persephone must spend six months with Pluto as Queen of Hades each year, but the other six she could return to earth.

Thus, says the story, during Summer and Autumn, Persephone is with her mother and the earth is lush and fruitful. However as the time for her to leave approaches, Demeter and all the trees and flowers droop, grief overcomes them and Autumn ends in mourning. During Winter, all is bleak and cold—there is no hope. But when Spring comes, the earth rejoices, preparing for Persephone's return with new growth and warmer days.

Why should we know about her?

The names and stories of Greek mythology crop up constantly in English language and literature. Daily newspapers or news commentators often refer to a Pandora's box, to Hades, or to someone's Achilles heel without giving background explanations. It's good to know what they're talking about and it's also interesting to compare Greek myths with those from other countries. That way we become more aware of the common bond that unites all peoples of the earth.

97

AND NOW A CURE FOR WINTER PROBLEMS:

A COMMERCIAL FOR SPRING

Eve Merriam

Tired of slush and snow and sleet?
Then try this dandy calendar treat!

You'll like the longer, king-size days;
You, too, will sing this season's praise.

It's the scientific sunshine pill
(Without that bitter winter chill).

It's naturally warmer, it's toasted through,
Exclusively mild for you and *you*.

It comes in the handy three-month pack:
March, April, May—or your money back.

So ask for S-P-R-I-N-
G, you'll never regret it;
Remember the name, its headed for fame:
Be the first on your block to get it!

THE STORY OF OPAL

Her parents died before she was five. She was given to an Oregon couple whose own child had died, and they named her Opal Whiteley. Because her foster father was a lumberman, Opal spent her childhood in 19 different lumber camps, where she started writing this diary in the early 1900s. She was then about five or six. When Opal was 12, a foster sister discovered the diary in its hiding place and tore the pages into thousands of pieces. Opal stored the pitiful scraps in a secret box.

Desperately poor at the age of 20, she tried to sell a nature book she had written to Ellery Sedgwick, the editor of Atlantic Monthly Press. Sedgwick asked if she had kept a diary of her interesting life. Opal burst into wordless tears. Then painfully, over nine months, she pieced together the shredded pages. In 1920, the diary was published as 'The Story of Opal' in a limited edition of 650 copies.

Jane Boulton

This story is an unusual one — one very different from the others in this book. We believe you will be touched by this account of an unhappy little foster child and the many problems she had to face after her parents died.

My mother and father are gone.
The man did say they went to Heaven and do live
with God, but it is lonesome without them.

The mamma where I live says I am a new sance.
I think it is something grown-ups don't like to have
around.
She sends me out to bring wood in.

Some days there is cream to be shaked into butter.
Some days I sweep the floor.
The mamma has likes to have her house nice and
clean.

Under the steps lives a toad.
I call him Virgil.
Under the house live some mice.
They have such beautiful eyes.
I give them bread to eat.

I like this house we do live in being at the edge of
the near woods.
All the way from the other logging camp in the
beautiful mountains we came in a wagon.
Two horses were in front of us.
They walked in front of us all the way.
When first we were come we did live with some
people in the ranch house that wasn't builded yet.
After that we lived in a tent.
Often when it did rain, many raindrops came right
through the tent.
They did fall in patters on the stove and on the floor
and on the table.
Too, they did make the quilts on the beds some
damp, but soon they got dried hanging around the
stove.

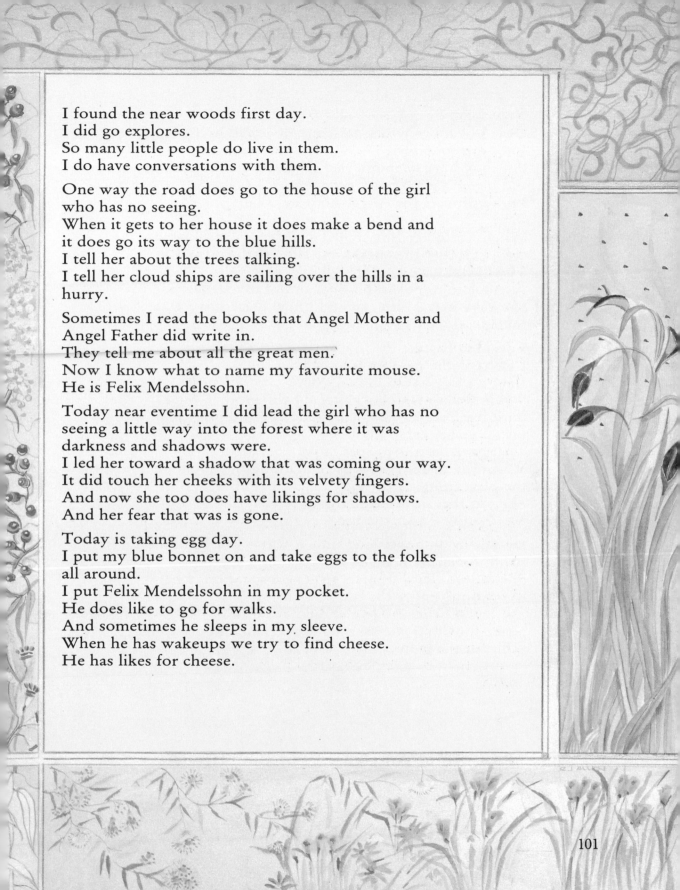

I found the near woods first day.
I did go explores.
So many little people do live in them.
I do have conversations with them.

One way the road does go to the house of the girl
who has no seeing.
When it gets to her house it does make a bend and
it does go its way to the blue hills.
I tell her about the trees talking.
I tell her cloud ships are sailing over the hills in a
hurry.

Sometimes I read the books that Angel Mother and
Angel Father did write in.
They tell me about all the great men.
Now I know what to name my favourite mouse.
He is Felix Mendelssohn.

Today near eventime I did lead the girl who has no
seeing a little way into the forest where it was
darkness and shadows were.
I led her toward a shadow that was coming our way.
It did touch her cheeks with its velvety fingers.
And now she too does have likings for shadows.
And her fear that was is gone.

Today is taking egg day.
I put my blue bonnet on and take eggs to the folks
all around.
I put Felix Mendelssohn in my pocket.
He does like to go for walks.
And sometimes he sleeps in my sleeve.
When he has wakeups we try to find cheese.
He has likes for cheese.

New folks live by the mill.
Dear Love, her young husband does call her.
They are so happy.
But they have been married seven whole months
and haven't got a baby yet.
I pray prayers for Angels to bring them one real
soon.
When I told her, she smiled glad smiles and kissed
me — two on the cheeks and one on the nose.
Then I did have joy feels all over and Felix
Mendelssohn poked his nose out of my sleeve.
She gave him a little pat and I new Dear Love was
my friend.

I decided to take the mother-pig for a walk.
I went to the woodshed.
I got a piece of clothesline rope.
While I was making a halter for the mother-pig I
took my Sunday-best hair ribbon — and put the bow
just over her ears.
That gave her the proper look.
When the mamma saw us go walking by, she took
the bow from off the pig.
She put that bow in the trunk.
Me she put under the bed.

By-and-by — some long time it was — she took me
from under the bed and did give me a spanking.
She did not have time to give me a spanking when
she put me under the bed.
She left me there until she did have time.
After she did it she sent me to the ranch house to get
milk for the baby.

I walked slow through the oak grove, looking for
caterpillars.
I found nine.

I sit here on the doorstep printing this on wrapping
paper.
The baby is in bed asleep.
The mamma and the rest of the folks is gone to the
ranch house.
She said for me to stay in the doorway to see that
nothing comes to carry the baby away.
The back part of me feels a little bit sore, but I am
happy listening to the twilight music of God's good
world.

The calf is Elizabeth Barrett Browning.
I think she will be a lovely cow.
Her mooings are musical and there is poetry in her
tracks.
She makes such dainty ones.
When they dry up in the lane I dig them up and
save them.
There are lonesome feels in her mooings when her
mother is away.
I put my arm around her neck.
It is such a comfort to have a friend near when
lonesome feels do come.

Jenny Strong visits the mamma.
All her plumpness fills the grey dress that she wears.
And every time she nods her head the pink rosebud
on her black bonnet gives itself a nod.
The mamma did spank me because I showed her my
mouse.
She sits by the fire and rocks and crochets.

She does make lace a quick way.
But I have wonders about her.
She does not like mice.

When I feel sad inside I talk things over with my
tree.
I call him Michael Raphael.
When I go off the barn roof it is a long jump into
his arms.
I might get my leg or my neck broken and I'd have
to keep still for a long time.
So I always say a little prayer and do jump in a
careful way.

It is such a comfort to nestle up to Michael Raphael.
He is a grand tree.
He has an understanding soul.

Today the grandpa dug potatoes in the field.
I followed along after.
I picked them up and piled them in piles.
Some of them were very plump.
And all the times I was picking up potatoes I did
have conversations with them.
Too, I did have thinks of all their growing days
there in the ground, and all the things they did hear.

Potatoes are very interesting folks.
I think they must see a lot of what is going on in the
earth.
They have so many eyes.
And after, I did count the eyes that every potato did
have, and their numbers were in blessings.

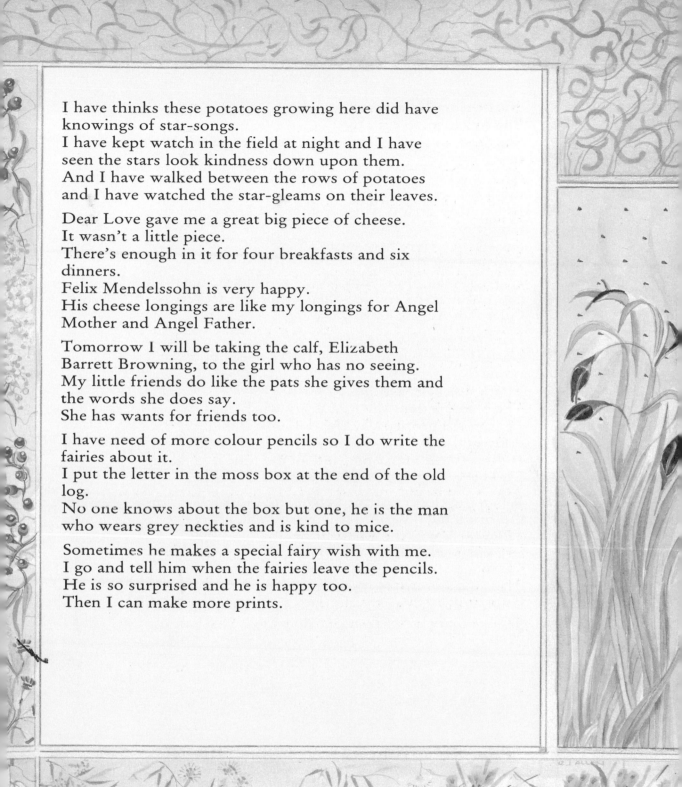

I have thinks these potatoes growing here did have
knowings of star-songs.
I have kept watch in the field at night and I have
seen the stars look kindness down upon them.
And I have walked between the rows of potatoes
and I have watched the star-gleams on their leaves.

Dear Love gave me a great big piece of cheese.
It wasn't a little piece.
There's enough in it for four breakfasts and six
dinners.
Felix Mendelssohn is very happy.
His cheese longings are like my longings for Angel
Mother and Angel Father.

Tomorrow I will be taking the calf, Elizabeth
Barrett Browning, to the girl who has no seeing.
My little friends do like the pats she gives them and
the words she does say.
She has wants for friends too.

I have need of more colour pencils so I do write the
fairies about it.
I put the letter in the moss box at the end of the old
log.
No one knows about the box but one, he is the man
who wears grey neckties and is kind to mice.

Sometimes he makes a special fairy wish with me.
I go and tell him when the fairies leave the pencils.
He is so surprised and he is happy too.
Then I can make more prints.

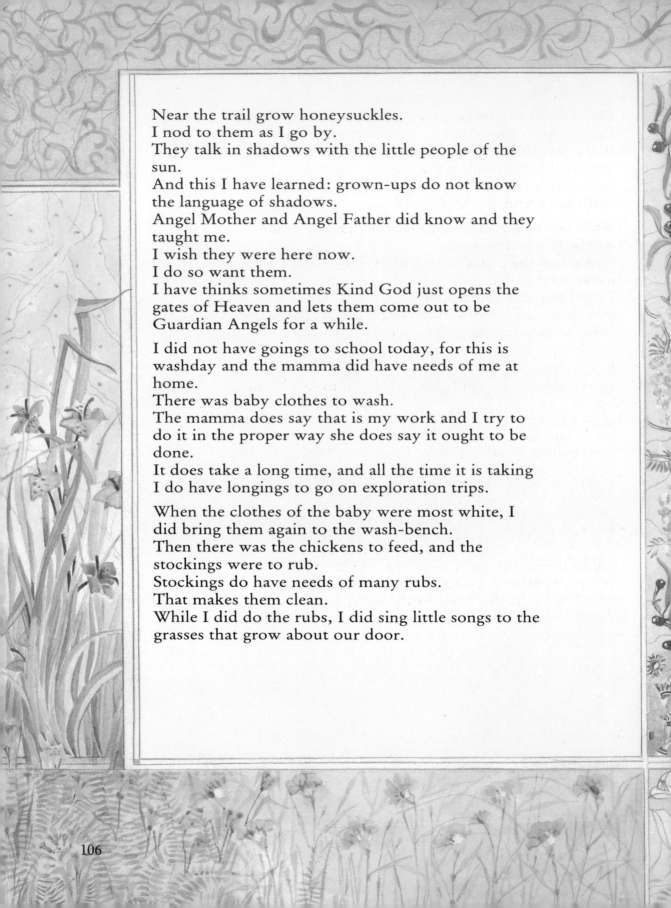

Near the trail grow honeysuckles.
I nod to them as I go by.
They talk in shadows with the little people of the sun.
And this I have learned: grown-ups do not know the language of shadows.
Angel Mother and Angel Father did know and they taught me.
I wish they were here now.
I do so want them.
I have thinks sometimes Kind God just opens the gates of Heaven and lets them come out to be Guardian Angels for a while.

I did not have goings to school today, for this is washday and the mamma did have needs of me at home.
There was baby clothes to wash.
The mamma does say that is my work and I try to do it in the proper way she does say it ought to be done.
It does take a long time, and all the time it is taking I do have longings to go on exploration trips.

When the clothes of the baby were most white, I did bring them again to the wash-bench.
Then there was the chickens to feed, and the stockings were to rub.
Stockings do have needs of many rubs.
That makes them clean.
While I did do the rubs, I did sing little songs to the grasses that grow about our door.

Today I went to Dear Love's house.
She was knitting socks for her husband.
I sat down beside her right near the blue gingham
apron with cross-stitches on it.
I counted thirty cross-stitches.
Some day I will count them all.

I went to the house of the girl who has no seeing
but she was not at home.
I did sit on the gatepost to wait waits.
It was a long time.
A man stopped and ask why I wait.
I told him and he looked off to the hills.
Then he did say, 'Child, she won't come back.'
I told him I knew she would come back because she
always does.
I gave him a sorry smile because he does not know
this.
I waited some more waits and then my mouse made
cheese squeaks.
I will go tomorrow.

Early this morning I went to the house of the girl
who has no seeing.
Two men were talking by the fence.
One did say, 'It is better so.'
The other man did say, 'A pit tea it was she
couldn't have the sight to see the bushfire ahead.'
Then, 'Probably the smell of the smoke caused her
to worry about the house with the fire coming.
Probably she was trying to find it when she walked
right into it.'

And the other man did have asks if she was con shus after.
He answered 'Yes.'

I felt a queerness in my throat and I couldn't see either.
More the men said.
They said all her clothes did have fire, and her running did make the fire to burn her more.
They found her when she died.

I go now to write a message on a leaf for the angels to carry her to Heaven and she can see the blooming flowers.
I will jump into Michael Raphael's arms and talk it over.

One of my tooths is loose and a queer feel.
The man who wears grey neckties and is kind to mice says tie a string around it on a doorknob.
I did as he said.
I started to walk off.
Then I came back aways.
I decided to wait a little while.
I walk off again.
Then I took the string off my tooth and thought I'd wait till after dinner.

One the way home from school I stop to get watercress for the mamma.
She does have such fondness for it.

Some days are long.
Some days are short.

The days that I have to stay in the house are the most long days of all.
There are no rows and rows and rows of books in this house like Angel Mother and Angel Father had.
There is only three books here.
One is a cook-book and one is a doctor-book and one is a almanac.
They are all on top of the cupboard most against the top of the house.

When the mowers cut down the grain they also do cut down the cornflowers that do grow in the fields.
I follow along after and do pick them up.
Of some I make a guirlande to put around Shakespeare's neck.
Then I do talk to him about the one he is named for.
He is such a beautiful grey horse and his ways are ways of gentleness.
Too he does have likings like the likings I have for the hills that are beyond the fields.

Some day I will write about the big tree that I love.
Today I watch and did hear its moans as the saw went through it.
There was a queer feel in my throat and I couldn't stand up.
When the saw did stop there was a stillness.
There was a queer sad sound.
The big tree did quiver.
It did sway.
It crashed to the earth.
Oh, Michael Raphael!

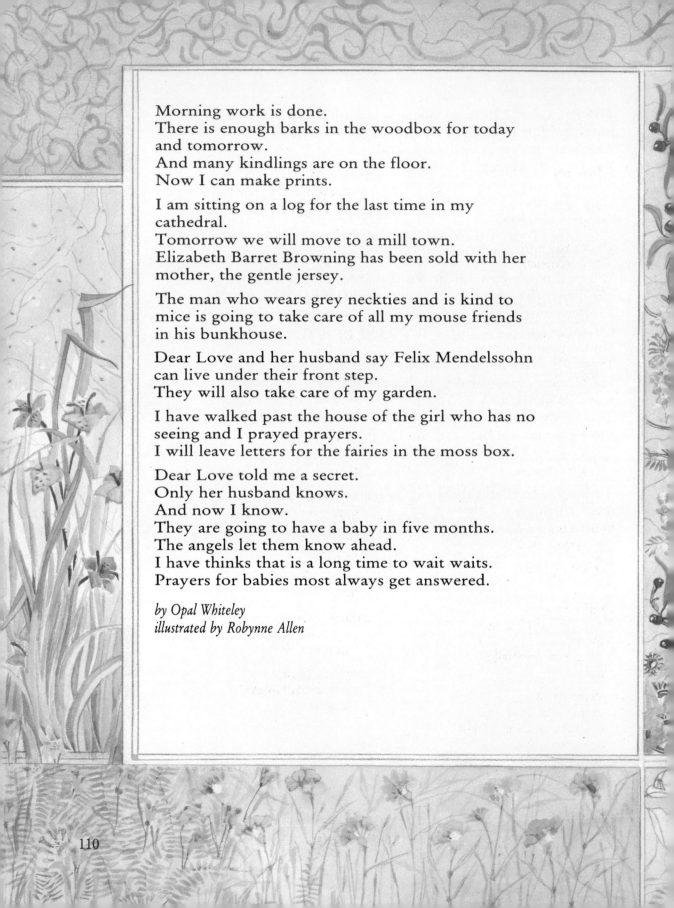

Morning work is done.
There is enough barks in the woodbox for today
and tomorrow.
And many kindlings are on the floor.
Now I can make prints.

I am sitting on a log for the last time in my
cathedral.
Tomorrow we will move to a mill town.
Elizabeth Barret Browning has been sold with her
mother, the gentle jersey.

The man who wears grey neckties and is kind to
mice is going to take care of all my mouse friends
in his bunkhouse.

Dear Love and her husband say Felix Mendelssohn
can live under their front step.
They will also take care of my garden.

I have walked past the house of the girl who has no
seeing and I prayed prayers.
I will leave letters for the fairies in the moss box.

Dear Love told me a secret.
Only her husband knows.
And now I know.
They are going to have a baby in five months.
The angels let them know ahead.
I have thinks that is a long time to wait waits.
Prayers for babies most always get answered.

by Opal Whiteley
illustrated by Robynne Allen

Words to work out

Glossary

acute *(p.34)*
keen

advocated *(p.70)*
recommended

almanac *(p.109)*
annual book containing
calendar, information on
stars and other facts

belligerent *(p.82)*
aggressive

brazier *(p.23)*
a metal stand to burn
coal in

chivalry *(p.69)*
honesty, bravery,
courtesy – the qualities of
a true knight

compelling *(p.24)*
powerful, forceful

diminutive *(p.28)*
tiny

distaffs *(p.43)*
rods with splits in them
for holding wool or flax,
wound for spinning by
hand

equinox *(p.88)*
time at which sun crosses
equator and day and night
are equal

ford *(p.66)*
cross a stream by wading

girdle *(p.68)*
belt

gouge *(p.20)*
force

guirlande *(p.109)*
garland, necklace

hoary *(p.42)*
ancient

inexplicably *(p.30)*
without explanation

inveigles *(p.73)*
tempts, persuades

lumberman *(p.99)*
forester, woodcutter

macabre *(p.73)*
grim, gruesome

mailed *(p.90)*
in armour

malice *(p.24)*
desire to harm

naturalist *(p.52)*
person who studies
animals or plants

oblivious *(p.38)*
not conscious of the
situation

Glossary continues on page 112

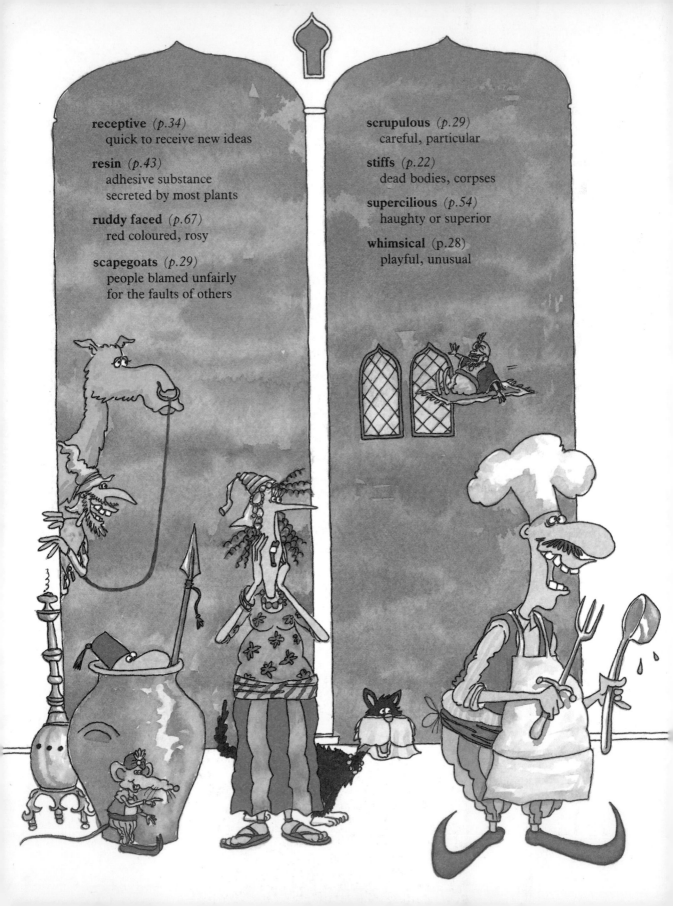

receptive *(p.34)*
quick to receive new ideas

resin *(p.43)*
adhesive substance
secreted by most plants

ruddy faced *(p.67)*
red coloured, rosy

scapegoats *(p.29)*
people blamed unfairly
for the faults of others

scrupulous *(p.29)*
careful, particular

stiffs *(p.22)*
dead bodies, corpses

supercilious *(p.54)*
haughty or superior

whimsical (p.28)
playful, unusual